CW00350984

Ireland

Ireland

Text by Ken Bernstein
Updated by Jason Mitchell
Photography: Doug Plummer
Cover Photo: Doug Plummer
Layout by Media Content Marketing, Inc.
Cartography by Ortelius Design
Managing Editor: Tony Halliday

Sixth Edition 2002

CONTACTING THE EDITORS

Every effort has been made to provide accurate information in this publication, but changes are inevitable. The publisher cannot be responsible for any resulting loss, inconvenience or injury. We would appreciate it if readers would call our attention to any errors or outdated information by contacting Berlitz Publishing, PO Box 7910, London SE1 1WE, England. Fax: (44) 20 7403 0290;
e-mail: berlitz@apaguide.demon.co.uk

CONTENTS

- A in the text denotes a highly recommended sight

Ireland

IRELAND AND THE IRISH

The grass grows greener in Ireland—it's not called the "Emerald Isle" for nothing, although the verdant pastures alternate with plains of grain, bleak, rugged hills, mountains, and soggy bogs. Yet the "Emerald Isle" is now more frequently referred to as the "Celtic Tiger," as the peaceful land of the leprechaun experiences its biggest economic boom in its independent history.

The quick-changing sky of this unspoiled Atlantic island only adds to the drama of the encounter between land and sea. You will never be farther than 113 km (70 miles) from Ireland's spectacular 4,800-km (3,000-mile) coastline rising from white sand coves to form some of Europe's most dramatic cliffs. Inland, at least one of the country's 800 lakes and rivers is usually within sight on this, the world's 20th largest island.

Though a species of palm tree thrives in many an Irish garden, you'd hardly mistake Ireland for a tropical paradise. Nonetheless, the proximity of the Gulf Stream keeps winter mild. Snow is rare, rain is not. Significant rainfall is recorded for about three out of every four days near the west coast, and for every second day in the east. The level of downpour varies enormously, and ranges from stormy torrents to refreshing mist that is so nebulous it leaves the pavement unmarked. The sun is never far behind the rain, however, and the slightest shower has always been a fine excuse for an Irish rainbow.

Sightseers who enjoy cities won't be disappointed, because in Dublin, a capital of broad avenues, green parks, and harmonious and ordered terraces, there is more in the way of museums, galleries, and other cultural attractions than in many cities its size. The River Liffey cuts through the heart of the city to the sea, and indeed all of Ireland's major towns derive their character from the sea or rivers or both. Belfast, the metropolis of the north, is Ireland's biggest port, while Cork, the Republic's second city, was founded in ages past by the Vikings on an island of the River Lee. In the west, the River Shannon explains and beautifies the city of Limerick.

By and large, however, the truly inspiring sights of Ireland are found outside of the big towns. Despite recent advancements in industry, Ireland continues to have an efficient agricultural foundation. As you travel by car or bus from one town to the next, you will pass through miles of farmland and are guaranteed a glimpse of many a flock of sheep. Natural wonders in Ireland can be as awesome as the Cliffs of Moher, or as tranquil as the Lakes of Killarney; as mystical as the "holy mountain" of Croagh Patrick, or as delightful as the horse-breeding prairie of the Curragh. Indeed, the mere concept of a town is not much more than a thousand years old. Before then Ireland was almost entirely rural and the most evocative parts of its ancient buildings were tranquil settlements of a monastic nature. In fact, the setting is more often than not an intrinsic part of the unique quality of the monument.

The great outdoors is where everything happens here. Between the rivers, the lakes and the sea, there's something exciting for every kind of fisherman. Sailing and boating share top billing. While the sea does not get any warmer than what might optimistically be called "refreshing," there'll be splashing about and sunbathing at hundreds of beaches. Of course, nobody could ever guarantee you a suntan in Ireland, but the beauty of the island, and the warmth of the people will certainly burn a place in your heart.

Scattered amidst the many natural beauties of the country stand impressive stone relics which date back thousands of years, while in the foreground, enhancing all the other attractions, are the handsome, hospitable people of Ireland. Meeting the locals is even easier when you forego the conventional hotel room and seek out accommodations in castles renovated as hotels, farmsteads, guesthouses, or quaint thatched cottages. The Irish call foreign travelers "visitors" rather than "tourists," and while the tourism industry is booming, they continue to offer a typically warm and generous "hundred thousand welcomes."

There are more than five million inhabitants on the island, and while that is still less than the number of residents 160 years ago, the country's population is finally on the rise. Over 1½ million live in Dublin; the largest city in the Republic of Ireland is home to more than 40% of its population. Young people abound both in the Republic and in Northern

Eat, drink, and be merry. Musicians and listeners enjoy a few pints at Centenary Stores Pub in County Wexford.

Ireland, which remained a part of the United Kingdom when the island was partitioned after World War I. The new generation finds Ireland in a period of great economic and social change. At the launch of the 21st century, the country is becoming secular, wealthy, and wired.

After more than nine centuries of suffering and the struggle for independence, the vitality of the new generation and the assistance of the European Union (EU) has allowed Ireland to make a complete turnaround from the economically-depressed nation that it once was. Tax incentives have lured various industries to the region, primarily in the high tech and pharmaceuticals sectors. In the last five years, the country has actually had more people emigrate to the coun-

All the pretty houses. Colorful cars, shops, and flats line the streets of Dingle in County Kerry.

try than leave, reversing a trend of immigration that has existed for over a century.

Despite the magnitude of the change that can be attributed to the help of the EU, the organization also plays a great part in the economic danger zone of the region. The Union is contemplating making sanctions against the tax incentives that originally attracted foreign business to the country. Unfortunately, the presence of the transnational corporations does not secure the future of Ireland. Like other countries that have been riding the economic wave of the late 1990s and early 2000s, the Celtic Tiger's prosperity could be greatly affected by fluctuating world markets.

The historic Anglo-Norman conquest of Ireland in the year 1169 paved the way for the supremacy of English over the colorful Gaelic. Nowadays barely one in a hundred people in Ireland speaks Irish more fluently than English. However, the revival of Gaelic, which is actually an Indo-European language, has become state policy; it is now taught in schools and printed (along with English) on all official signs and documents.

The old Ireland still exists all about the lush green countryside, but everyday use of Gaelic in practice is limited to the Gaeltacht areas—the small pockets of culture predominantly in the west of the island. Its vocabulary and intonation have molded the distinctive, lilting form of English spoken throughout the country. Eloquence in English is not merely confined to great Irish authors and playwrights (after all this is the land of Joyce, Wilde, Shaw, Sheridan, and Beckett); almost everybody in Ireland seems to be a witty, articulate conversationalist. Many people who live in the cities (and many smaller towns) also speak the language of modernity and technology. You'll find cybercafés and cyberpubs scattered about the country, both in the Republic and in Northern Ireland.

Leisure sport of the future? The road bowlers of County Cork stand proud on Enniskean Road.

The six counties of Northern Ireland have seen a truly remarkable resurgence in recent years. The area has received the greatest subsidy from Britain, the EU, and the International Fund for Ireland (IFI), which consists primarily of contributions from the US. The economy in the north has seen a steady increase for the last twenty years. Despite the tumultuous history in the area, violence has decreased tremendously, resulting in a rapid rise in tourism. With an influx of computer software companies, unemployment levels have dipped and the future is looking bright for Northern Ireland.

A jewel of an island, nestled between the Atlantic Ocean and the Irish and Celtic Seas, Ireland is one of Europe's finest (and increasingly flourishing) destinations.

A BRIEF HISTORY

As with all the great, timeless sagas, the story of Ireland is propelled on waves of tragedy, challenge, and adventure. For the Irish of today, ancient legends are as close as yesterday, and historic crises as topical as this morning's headlines.

Relics from the Stone Age lead to the general conclusion that Ireland has been inhabited for at least 8,000 years. The first settlers here may well have even traveled on foot from Scandinavia to Scotland—England was linked at that time to northern Europe by land—then across what was a narrow sea gap to Ireland.

During the later phase of the Stone Age, the inhabitants settled down as farmers. Tombs and temples from this period can be found in many parts of the country, usually in the

The Dromberg Stone Circle near Rosscarbery is one of many mysterious monuments from the Stone Age.

middle of somebody's pasture. Some of the monuments are merely stone tripods; others, though, are as sophisticated as neolithic passage-graves, built on principles of astronomical alignment, containing strange engravings in spiral and zigzag patterns that had meaning for their creators.

Although new settlers and contacts with Europe brought along Bronze Age skills, Ireland still lagged behind the Continent in the next big revolution—the Iron Age. This technology finally reached the island during the last years of the pre-Christian era, brought in by tribes who originated in central Europe. Fighters truly worthy of legend, the language they spoke was Celtic.

The Roman legions that rolled across western Europe stopped short at the Irish Sea. This helps to explain why the Irish are so different: they developed their own way of life during the formative centuries of the great Roman Empire. Though Irish society was hopelessly decentralized—the sparse population widely dispersed under the sway of scores of bickering mini-kingdoms—a single culture did develop. Druids and poets told legends in a common language, one that was clearly recognizable as the Irish version of Gaelic.

St. Patrick's Day

From time to time, the Celts staged raids on Roman Britain for booty and slaves. During one fifth-century raid, the tough Irish commandos rounded up a large number of captives to ease the manpower shortage. One of these "immigrants," a 16-year-old boy named Patrick, was later to become the national saint. After a few years spent as a simple shepherd, he escaped to Gaul, heard the call of his life's mission, became a monk, and finally returned to Ireland in order to convert heathens to Christianity.

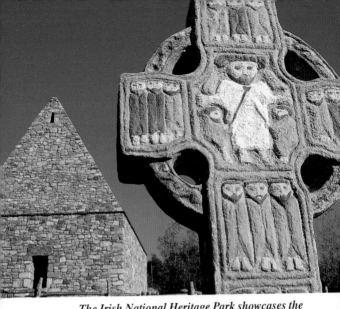

The Irish National Heritage Park showcases the country's early Christian iconography.

St. Patrick's crusade was a unique triumph—for Ireland is the only Western European country where the surrender of the pagans was achieved without a single Christian being martyred.

One of St. Patrick's great innovations was the system of monasteries around which all church activities centered. This was suited to life in Ireland, a rural and skimpily populated island with its diverse power blocs. While the rest of Europe crawled on through the Dark Ages, the flame of Western culture was kept alight in Irish monasteries. The monks of the "island of saints and scholars" dutifully copied manuscripts from civilization; some of the books

were so beautiful that they qualify as major works of art.
The early Irish church leaders also founded an active missionary tradition.

The first great Irishman to propagate the faith beyond
the sea was Colmcille, a scholarly poet of the sixth century
who founded the Iona Monastery near the coast of Scotland, and converted the Picts to Christianity. Young Colmcille, or St. Columba, was succeeded by St. Columbanus,
whose long odyssey took him through France, Switzerland, Austria, and Italy. At this time, scholarly minds from
different regions of Europe converged on the island in
order to participate in its diverse and active religious and
intellectual life.

The Vikings

At the turn of the ninth century, the security of Irish society was imperilled by tough and hardy intruders from the
north. Well-armed warriors sailed in from Scandinavia
aboard sleek boats in search of booty. The Irish monasteries holding their relics and treasures were easy targets for
the Vikings. Their shallow-draught ships moved in and
attacked virtually at will all around the Irish coast and up
rivers as well.

The danger and uncertainty of the era inspired the design
of multi-storey "round towers." Dozens of these combination watch-towers, belfries, storehouses, and escape hatches
are still standing. In most of them the entrance was built
high above ground level so the ladder could be hauled up at
the first glimpse of a Norse sail.

Soon the sea traffic became constructive, with the Vikings
adding trading colonies around the coast. It was the Vikings
who founded the first towns on the rural island—Dublin,
Waterford, and Limerick.

The Irish learned sailing, weaponry, and metalworking from the Norse, but this did nothing to help the fact that their presence always rankled. Finally the natives ousted the Vikings, with the final struggle in the year 1014 at the Battle of Clontarf, when the High King of Ireland, Brian Boru, took on the tough Norse as well as their Irish allies. Boru was killed, but not before he had defeated the Vikings.

Cherchez La Femme

Behind the next invasion of Ireland lay many motivations, including jealousy. This tale begins in 1152, when the wife of Tiernan O'Rourke, one of the Irish warrior-kings, was carried off by a rival, Dermot MacMurrough of Leinster. It is alleged that the lady was a willing victim—in fact possibly even the instigator, but whichever the case, O'Rourke got his queen back a few months later.

However, being the kind of man he was, he wasn't about to forgive and forget.

O'Rourke and his allies put so much military pressure on King Dermot that in 1166 he fled first to England and then France. Dermot then shaped an alliance with a powerful Norman nobleman, the Earl of Pembroke. The Earl, known as Strongbow, agreed to lead an army to sweep Dermot back to power. The other half of the bargain struck was that the Earl would be given the hand of Dermot's daughter, and the right to succeed him to the Leinster throne. In the event, the hardy Normans—the élite of Europe's warriors—won the Battle of Waterford in 1169, and even before the raging flames of the battle had been extinguished, Strongbow married his heart's desire, the princess, in Waterford's grand cathedral.

In further engagements, the Norman war machine stunned and swiftly defeated the Norse and Irish forces. Indeed things were going so well for Strongbow that his overlord, King Henry of England, arrived on the scene in 1171 to assert his sovereignty.

Gael and Pale

The protracted Anglo-Norman occupation inevitably brought with it profound and long-lasting changes. Towns, churches and castles were built, and institutions for feudal government were created. Ireland was never totally conquered, however: The Irish identity was undiluted, and resistance and resentment persisted.

For the colonial rulers, the challenge of revolt was less serious than the danger of total cultural assimilation.

With the settlers adopting the ways of the natives, rather than the other way round, an attempt to enforce a form of apartheid was launched with the Statutes of Kilkenny (in 1366) introduced in order to forbid intermarriage and ban the Gaelic language. English was spoken only in the Pale, that area around Dublin where the occupation forces were in command.

English control of Ireland was not actually consolidated until the grand House of Tudor turned its attention to Ireland, making it a training ground for the empire. King Henry VIII was the first English monarch to adopt the new title "King of Ireland." Following his break with Rome, he attempted to introduce the Reformation to Ireland as well as England, but the new religion only had real influence in the Pale and in the large provincial towns under English control. In the rest of Ireland, the monasteries and the Catholicism they sought to nurture carried on as before, and so did the Irish language.

In the middle of the 16th century, the implementation of the so-called plantation policy pointed the way to large-scale redistribution of wealth as well as to the complete suppression of Catholicism. Desirable farm land was quickly confiscated from Catholics and given to Protestant settlers.

The hard Tudor conquest of Ireland ultimately required plenty of well-organised military armed force, and during the reign of Queen Elizabeth I, two major revolts had to be stopped. Throughout, the most unyielding resistance was in the province of Ulster. The Ulster chiefs, led by Hugh O'Neill, tried one last ploy—alliance with Queen Elizabeth's bitterest enemy, Spain. In 1601, a Spanish mini-armada sailed into the southern port of Kinsale. The English defeated the invaders and the Ulstermen who attempted to join them; but O'Neill, along with the leading Ulster aristocrats, soon abandoned their land for European exile. But the "plantation" program went on in fits and starts. Most of the land of the north was swiftly confiscated and "planted" with thousands of Scots and English, who made the province of Ulster forever different. After 1654, Catholics were only allowed to hold land to the west of the River Shannon, much of it scarcely habitable. "To Hell or Connaught" was the slogan used to express the alternatives for the dispossessed.

Religious War

Events in England had their most violent repercussions in the mid-17th century. Oliver Cromwell arrived in Dublin soon after Charles I was executed, and supervised a campaign against those who had supported the king, in which the towns of Drogheda and Wexford were special targets for destruction. By the time Cromwell left Ireland in 1650, the backbone of resistance had been broken.

Ireland again became a hard battleground when William of Orange, a Protestant, and now a culturally significant figure

A 1798 commemorative statue stands tall in New Ross, County Wexford.

in English history, challenged his father-in-law, the Catholic James II, over the succession to the British throne. From his exile in France, James sailed to Ireland in order to mobilize his allies. William promptly came over from England for the showdown in July 1690, which is known as the Battle of the Boyne.

The Orangemen, aided by troops from several Protestant countries, vastly outnumbered the combined Irish and French forces commanded by James. As momentous battles go, it set no records either for scope nor for tactical innovation. Nor did it end the war as the losers fled to regroup. William of Orange was the winner of the Battle of the Boyne, and today its anniversary is celebrated with fervor by Protestants in Northern Ireland.

When the war finally ended with the Treaty of Limerick in 1691, the religious rights of Catholics were guaranteed. It comes as no surprise that the all-Protestant Irish parliament soon passed a series of "Penal Laws" to keep all positions of power and influence well out of reach of the Catholic majority.

Revolutionary Ideas

The colonists' victory in the American Revolution sparked off daring and new thinking in Ireland. Agitation for greater freedom and tolerance was led by Henry Grattan, a Protestant of aristocratic heritage, who staunchly defended the rights of all Irishmen in the House of Commons in London. Some restrictions were eased a little and so Ireland won a limited measure of autonomy.

Further pressure in this field came from the Irish Protestant, Theobald Wolfe Tone, a young lawyer campaigning for parliamentary reform and abolition of the anti-Catholic laws. British government tried to ban Wolfe Tone's supporters, the United Irishmen—but in 1793 Catholics won the vote as well as other concessions for which he fought. Five years later, with the United Irishmen in rebellion, a French squadron came to their aid off the coast of Donegal and was swiftly intercepted by the British naval forces.

Wolfe Tone was captured on board the flagship of the fleet; he was wearing the uniform of a French officer. Convicted of treason, he committed suicide before his sentence could be carried out.

In 1801 the Irish Parliament was abolished. It voted itself out of business after approving the Act of Union which established the United Kingdom of Great Britain and Ireland. All Irish politicians would now sit with MPs at Westminster, and thus the Mother of Parliaments was to govern Ireland from afar. The idea behind this shift was for the economic and political destinies of the two islands to become inseparable, but Irish nationalism has never really faded away.

A leading opponent of the act was Daniel O'Connell, one of the first Catholics ever to gain admission to the Irish Bar.

In 1823 he founded the Catholic Association, a mass-movement working for emancipation. He won a landslide victory only five years later in a by-election for the House of Commons, but as a Catholic he was paradoxically legally forbidden to take his seat. To quench more conflict, Parliament swiftly passed the Emancipation Act (1829), in which the most discriminative laws were removed. Subsequently, O'Connell tried to gain the repeal of the Act of Union, and although he failed, he is today remembered in Ireland as "The Liberator."

Starvation and Emigration

One of the worst disasters of 19th-century Europe was the great Irish famine.

The first hint of a problem was in September 1845, when the disease potato blight was discovered on farms in southeast Ireland. The British government immediately set up an investigation, but the outbreak was not diagnosed correctly. The next crop was a disaster nationwide and the staple food of the Irish peasant totally disappeared. Cruel winter weather and an inevitable outbreak of disease added to the horror of starvation.

The survivors stampeded to flee the stricken land aboard creaking "coffin ships." Pitiful Irish refugees swamped towns such as Liverpool, Halifax, Boston, and New York. The toll of the famine is estimated to have reduced the population of Ireland by two million; half of them died, and the rest emigrated. It took another century before the constant decline in the population figures was redressed, and the flow of emigrants was stemmed.

Emigrants were among the founders of the Irish Republican Brotherhood—the Fenian movement—a broadly based secret organization dedicated to overthrowing

British rule. An IRB uprising in 1867 was crushed, but the survivors regrouped and planned a very successful revolt. They had to wait some 49 years for their big chance.

In the last part of the 19th century, two different Irishmen led a major campaign to return the land to the peasants. The first of these, Michael Davitt, was the founder of the Land League. He was a revolutionary who had a normal, working-class background, and one arm. The other, Charles Stewart Parnell, who became the Land League's president, was a Member of Parliament of the Protestant upper class.

Together they declared the famous "land war" of 1879-1882, in which great masses of the people became involved. The struggle finally brought down the landlord structure. In one incident, a County Mayo land agent just refused to grant his cooperation to the reformers. The Land League cut him off from the rest of the world so well that the name of the man, Charles Boycott, passed into English as the common word for an organized snub.

Frustration and Revolt

At the end of the 19th century a series of frustrations beset the forces for Irish autonomy or home rule. Charles Parnell, the shining hope of the Irish cause, lost influence once he was convicted of adultery said to have been committed with the wife of a fellow Member of Parliament. New home rule legislation was pushed through the Commons, but it was rejected in the Lords.

Nationalist sentiment was encouraged, and manifested itself in the formation of such groups as Gaelic Athletic Association and the Gaelic League. In 1905 a number of nationalist groups were consolidated in a new movement called Sinn Féin (which is Irish for "ourselves alone").

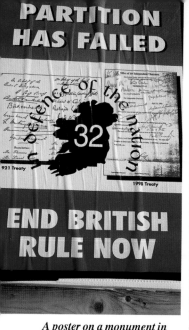

A poster on a monument in Cork City is a peaceful reminder of Nationalist views.

Legislation for home rule looked more abstract than ever when Britain entered World War I, and so activists decided that the time would never be more apt for an uprising.

The Easter Rising of 1916 saw rebels seize the General Post Office in Dublin, and in a symbolic gesture they proclaimed it as a new government for the Irish Republic. The authorities soon crushed this move, which had in any case lacked general support, but the fast and pitiless repression which sent the leaders to the firing squad shocked the people and paved the way for the war of independence.

At the next general election the nationalist Sinn Féin, now led by Eamon de Valera, won by a landslide. De Valera, born in New York City of an Irish mother and a Spanish father, had been a commander during the Easter Rising.

Two Irelands

The newly elected Sinn Féin parliamentarians refused to fill their posts in the Commons in London, but instead set themselves up in Dublin as Dáil Éireann, the new parliament of Ireland.

There followed more than two years of guerrilla warfare and reprisals by the government until finally the crisis was cooled by the partition of Ireland which took place in December 1921. Under it, six counties of the north, where the majority of the population was Protestant and opposed to rule from Dublin, remained part of the United Kingdom. The other 26 counties were of Catholic majority, and became the Irish Free State, a dominion existing within the British Empire.

Fervent republicans rejected partition and partial links with Britain, and unleashed a civil war commonly known as "The Troubles" which shook the brand new state. Among the many casualties of nearly a year's hard fighting was Michael Collins, the commander of the provisional government's armed forces and a legendary independence fighter; he was killed in an ambush in August 1922.

Eire, the new country, progressively loosened ties with Britain, with the most conclusive demonstration being Ireland's neutrality in World War II. After the war, the new Republic was admitted to the UN and so undertook a new, international role, providing troops for peace-keeping operations.

As Britain and Ireland joined the EEC (now the European Union), hopes bloomed that both countries could work more closely together, but the road to peace in Northern Ireland has seemed at times endless and always complicated. In 1994, fresh hopes were kindled when the Irish Republican Army (IRA) declared a ceasefire. Protestant paramilitaries followed shortly afterwards with an equal commitment. The Good Friday Agreement, in 1998, then established the framework for a self-governing Northern Ireland and began a peaceful period that has recently disintegrated among some of the worst violence and in-fighting since "The Troubles" began.

WHERE TO GO

Y ou can't see it all. Ireland's geographic surface area may be modest, but it contains too many worthwhile sights to see in a single vacation. It would take three weeks simply to try out all the different day trips run by CIE (Tel. 01 703-4676; web site <www.cietours.ie>), the national Irish transport company. Big decisions have to be made on what to see, and they will all depend on how much time you have, what you prefer to see, and how you're traveling.

The best way to see Ireland is by car, though various fly-drive package deals or bus tours exist as an alternative. You can see a large proportion of Ireland using public transport, although apart from the main routes, the bus schedules tend to be designed more for country folk than tourists.

Ancient Ireland was divided into four provinces: Leinster (including Dublin); Munster in the southwest; the rugged grandeur of westernmost Connacht; and to the north Ulster, with its striking coastline.

This book covers the high-spots of Ireland roughly in that order, starting in Dublin and proceeding more or less clockwise. We cannot describe all the sights—or even all the counties—but wherever you go, you'll enjoy Ireland more at an Irish pace.

DUBLIN

The capital of Ireland (population over 1 million–Greater Dublin) is the birthplace and inspiration of many great authors, as well as a very European city with low-profile buildings—many of them truly outstanding examples of 18th-century architecture.

Dublin is pervaded by contrasting moods which affect even transient visitors; from its noble avenues and intimate side streets to chic shopping and old smoky pubs, there are also museums, colleges, and plenty of sports. In this melting pot of old and new, traditional lace still masks modern windows and policemen on bicycles report in by lapel radio.

The city's name comes from the Irish *Dubhlinn*, meaning "a dark pool," and a much older Gaelic name on buses and signs—*Baile Atha Cliath*, "the town of the hurdle ford"—explains why Dublin was originally settled: it was a place to ford the River Liffey.

The river, with its tranquil canals and the entrance it provides to the Irish Sea nearby, contributes much to the atmosphere. Seagulls frequent the center of town, as do the ghosts of marauding Vikings, Normans, and Viceroys... as well as Leopold and Molly Bloom, late of Eccles Street.

The Must-See Sights

Achill Island cliffs and beaches, County Mayo (see page 81)

Aran Islands (see page 76)

Ben Bulben mountain and W.B. Yeats' grave, County Sligo (see page 82)

Burren, County Clare (lunar landscape, many unique species of flora—see page 72)

Dingle Peninsula (see page 66)

Dublin's 18th-century Georgian district (see page 31)

Giant's Causeway, County Antrim (see page 85)

Glendalough (see page 46)

Mourne Mountains (see page 85)

Newgrange prehistoric site, County Meath (see page 41)

Phoenix Park, Dublin (see page 38)

Ring of Kerry drive (see page 64)

Rock of Cashel, County Tipperary (see page 52)

Twelve Bens mountains, Co. Galway (see page 78)

West Cork (see page 62)

O'Connell Street to St. Stephen's Green

The main street in Dublin is **O'Connell Street**, worthy of a major capital, and a lasting monument to the Wide Street Commissioners of the early 1800s. Measuring 46 m (150 ft) across, it is straight as the morals of Father Theobald Mathew, the deeply admired 19th-century priest known as the Apostle of Temperance, who is commemorated in one of the four monuments down the middle of the road. There used to be five, but as a strong anti-British gesture in 1966, anonymous citizens planned a removal of the Nelson Pillar, erected in 1808. Some Dubliners still admire the daring of the crew that blew it up in the middle of the night.

The most famous landmark on O'Connell Street is the **General Post Office**, which has a significance far greater than its postal predominance. The GPO was the command post of the 1916 Easter Rising and was badly damaged in the fighting. A plaque on the front of the building, in Irish and English, and the statue inside mark the historic event.

To the south, just opposite O'Connell Bridge, is the large and complex monument honoring "The Liberator," Daniel O'Connell (1775-1847), and after whom both the street and bridge are named.

From the bridge, almost as wide as it is long, you can look up and down the **River Liffey** and along the embankments. To the east, beyond the skyscraper-style headquarters of the Irish trade unions, rises the copper dome of the majestic 18th-century **Custom House**. Like many buildings along the River Liffey, it was all but destroyed in the civil war fighting of 1921, but has now been magnificently restored to its present gleaming white.

Some of the most interesting old buildings, including a few disused churches, are now occupied by banks, but it may come as a surprise to learn that the momentous white building facing College Green on the south side of the River Liffey is a branch of the **Bank of Ireland** company. It was built in the 18th century to house parliament, but when parliament was abruptly abolished by the Act of Union in 1801 (see page 21), the bank moved in. The portico has 22 Ionic columns.

Behind the railings at the entrance to **Trinity College** are the statues of two famous alumni—philosopher Edmund Burke and playwright Oliver Goldsmith. Founded by Queen Elizabeth I in 1592, Trinity is a timeless enclave of calm and scholarship in the middle of this bustling city. For centuries it was seen as an exclusively Protestant institution, and as recently as 1956 the Catholic church forbade its students to attend Trinity "under pain of mortal sin." Today, TCD, as it is called, is integrated.

Most of the campus forms a monument to the good taste of the 18th century, and visitors enjoy cobbled walks

*An Irish Parliament was once housed in the prodigious
Bank of Ireland on College Street.*

Trinity College is a bustling, modern university on a lovely, historic campus.

amongst trimmed lawns, fine old trees, statues, and stone buildings. You can also enjoy the Dublin Experience here, an audiovisual show on the city's history.

The greatest treasures are in the vaulted Long Room in the **Old Library**, where double-decker shelving holds thousands of books published prior to 1800, and priceless early manuscripts are displayed in glass cases.

In the adjacent Colonnades Gallery lines of students and tourists reverently wait for a look at the **Book of Kells**. This 340-page parchment wonder, hand-written and illustrated by monks during the ninth century, contains a Latin version of the New Testament. The beauty of the script, the illumination (the decoration of initial letters and words) and the bright abstract designs—above all the saintly portraits—constitute the most wonderful treasure to survive from Ireland's Golden Age. The vellum leaves are turned every day to protect them from the light and to give visitors a chance to come back for more.

Examples of Europe's finest Georgian houses can be seen facing **Merrion Square**, once the proposed site for a Catholic cathedral and now a park. The discreet, smart brick houses have those Dublin doorways flanked by tall columns and topped by fanlights. No two are alike. In a complex of formal buildings on the west side of the square, stands the city's largest 18th-century mansion, home of the Duke of Leinster. Today **Leinster House** is the seat of the Irish parliament, which consists of the Senate (*Seanad Éireann*) and the Chamber of Deputies (the *Dáil*, which is pronounced "doyle").

Standing at the entrance to the **National Gallery** you will see a statue of George Bernard Shaw, famous and respected Dubliner known locally as a benefactor of the institution.

In the **National Gallery** (web site <www.nationalgallery. ie>) some 2,000 works of art are displayed, but 6,000 more are held in reserve. Irish artists receive priority, but other nation-alities are also well represented, such as Dutch, English, Flemish, French, Italian, and Spanish masters. Among those on display are, in chronological order: Fra Angelico, Rubens, Rembrandt, Canaletto, Gainsborough, and Goya. In addition, rounding off what is a prize collection of medieval religious art, the gallery has two treasured frescoes dating from the 11th or 12th century, delicately lifted from the walls of the Chapel of St. Pierre-de-Campublic in Beaucaire, France.

The main entrance to the **National Museum**, a Dublin in-stitution, is reached from Kildare Street. The museum's col-lection of Irish antiquities contains several surprises, from old skeletons and tools to exquisite gold ornaments of the Bronze Age. The most famous items on display include the eighth-century Ardagh Chalice, the delicate Tara Brooch from the same era, and the 12th-century Shrine of St. Patrick's Bell.

A WAY WITH WORDS

Storytelling comes naturally to the Irish. Ireland's rich literary heritage is brought to life in the Dublin Writers Museum (18-19 Parnell Square North), where fixed displays are complemented with lectures, readings, and talks. There is also a Living Writers Center, where visiting writers are welcome, and a children's section, where storytimes are held.

Here are some of Ireland's greatest authors.

Jonathan Swift (1667-1745), a satirist and the dean of St. Patrick's Cathedral. Writing was only a part-time job for the romantic clergyman best remembered for *Gulliver's Travels.*

Oliver Goldsmith (c. 1728-1774) studied medicine, then entered the London circle of Dr. Samuel Johnson. He wrote the novel *The Vicar of Wakefield*, the play *She Stoops to Conquer*, and the poem *The Deserted Village.*

Oscar Wilde (1854-1900). His haunting, original novel, *The Picture of Dorian Gray*, was followed by witty comedies like *The Importance of Being Earnest.* Imprisoned on a charge of homosexual conduct, he wrote *The Ballad of Reading Gaol.*

George Bernard Shaw (1856-1950), Dublin-born, spent most of his life in England. *Arms and the Man, Man and Superman*, and *Pygmalion* made him the greatest dramatist of the age. Shaw was also an inveterate controversialist.

William Butler Yeats (1865-1939), like Shaw, won the Nobel prize. His poems sang the glories of Ireland. A founder of the Abbey Theatre and senator of the young Irish Free State.

Sean O'Casey (1880-1964), wrote tragi-comedy—*The Shadow of a Gunman, Juno and the Paycock*, and *The Plough and the Stars*. His later plays were less successful.

James Joyce (1882-1941) re-created Dublin in his imagination from European exile. *Ulysses*, his revolutionary stream-of-consciousness novel in a Homeric framework, was banned in Ireland (and elsewhere) during his lifetime.

You can also see ancient Ogham stones. Much of the collection has moved to the former Collins army barracks site, near Heuston station.

If you don't have time to make a full tour of churchyards and far-off monasteries, you can admire many replicas of the greatest carved stone crosses from early centuries of Christian Ireland.

The southeastern part of central Dublin is handsomely and unusually well endowed with breathing space, thanks to a number of pleasant squares and parks. The biggest of these —and possibly the biggest city square in Europe—is the famous **St. Stephen's Green**. During the 18th century the square was almost completely surrounded by elegant town houses. Some survive today, though many conservationists despair at the rapidly declining number. Inside the square is a perfectly delightful park with pretty flower gardens and a man-made lake inhabited by waterfowl. Among the many sculptures and monuments in varied styles there is also a memorial to the poet and playwright W.B. Yeats by Henry Moore. Nearby is also a bust to commemorate Yeats' friend who is today seen as an historic figure, the Countess Constance Markievicz, who defended the square during the 1916 insurrection, and who was the first woman elected to the British House of Commons.

Another statue honors the man who paid for landscaping the square: Lord Ardilaun, son of the founder of the Guinness brewery. Some thirsty sightseers might be inspired to find a nearby pub and raise a toast to the stout-hearted benefactor.

Medieval Dublin

Dublin Castle was begun in the 13th century, set on a hill high above the original Viking settlement on the south bank of the River Liffey. It was rebuilt during the 18th century, which explains why it no longer looks like a medieval castle. Over the years it has served as a seat of government, as a prison, a courthouse, and occasionally as a fortress under siege—most recently in 1916. Many visiting heads of state have been fêted in the lavish State Apartments, which were once the grand residence of the British Viceroy.

Around the corner from the castle stands the **City Hall** (in former times the Royal Exchange). Built during the late 18th century in solid, classical style, it contains an interesting collection of royal charters and municipal regalia.

Dublin has not one but two noteworthy cathedrals to offer, and although it is the official capital of what is a predominantly Catholic country, both of the cathedrals belong to the Protestant Church of Ireland. The reason for two cathedrals is easily explained if you have the time to sift through the various historic, political and religious rivalries which had an effect here.

Dublin Castle's Upper Yard houses the magnificent State Apartments, today used for government functions.

In any case, **Christ Church** Cathedral is the older of the two, dating from 1038. One unusual architectural touch is the covered pedestrian bridge over Winetavern Street, which links the church and its Synod Hall. This was built during the Victorian era, but doesn't spoil the overall mood. Otherwise, Christ Church cathedral boasts Romanesque, as well as Early English, and fine Neo-Gothic elements.

If you would like to delve more deeply into Irish history, you could visit novel Dublinia, which is in the Synod Hall of the cathedral. This is an impressive multimedia heritage center depicting how Dubliners lived in the medieval city, offering Viking artefacts and a closing audiovisual show.

The crypt, which runs under the full length of the church, rather like a vast wine cellar, is a surviving remnant from the 12th century, during which the cathedral was expanded by Strongbow (see page 17), whose mortal remains lie buried here. Although it has been regarded as authentic for many decades, modern scholars are in heated debate about the authenticity of the Strongbow tomb.

You can see the fine statue of a recumbent cross-legged knight in full armor in the southern aisle.

A short walk south from Christ Church Cathedral leads to Dublin's newer and larger cathedral, **St. Patrick's**, which is dedicated to Ireland's national saint. It is said that St. Patrick himself baptized fifth-century converts at a well on this very site; indeed, a stone slab used for covering the well can be found in the northwest of the cathedral. This church was consecrated in 1192, but the present architectural structure dates mostly from the 13th and 14th centuries. The cathedral is known for its association with the writer Jonathan Swift, the famous crusading satirist, who was appointed dean in 1713, and served until his death in 1745. Many Swiftian relics can be seen in a corner of the north transept, and a simple brass plate in the

Historic St. Patrick's Cathedral, where Jonathan Swift was dean for 32 years.

floor near the entrance marks his grave. Next to this you can see the tomb of the mysterious Stella, one of the two great loves of his life. Above the lintel of the robing room you can read his own bitter epitaph, written in Latin: "Savage indignation can no longer gnaw his heart. Go, traveler, and imitate, if you can, this earnest and dedicated defender of liberty."

The talented choirboys of St. Patrick's Cathedral lift up their voices—and the hearts of listeners—at the services given every day of the week except on Saturdays. A joint choir formed from both cathedrals was the first to sing Handel's *Messiah* when the composer was in Dublin in 1742. A copy from the year 1799 can be seen in Marsh's Library, Ireland's first public library, founded in 1701.

Temple Bar is a city area that runs from Westmoreland Street to Christ Church Cathedral. With its 18th and 19th century architecture, major developments are aimed at turning the area into the arts and crafts quarter of Dublin. The Irish Film Center is now complete and open to the public, as is the Viking Museum. Temple Bar is a good area to consider for dining out.

The North Bank

The most impressive building located on the north bank of the Liffey is the domed home of the **Four Courts** (originally the Chancery, Common Pleas, Exchequer, and King's Bench). This is the magnificent work of James Gandon, the respected 18th-century English-born architect who also designed Dublin's Custom House. The courthouse was quite seriously damaged by the consistent and prolonged shelling during the 1922 civil war. After lengthy reconstruction, however, it was restored, and justice continues to be dispensed in the Neoclassic Four Courts. Carrying on the tradition which was introduced by the British, Irish lawyers in action wear wigs and gowns when in Superior Courts.

St. Michan's Church, just around the corner in Church Street, was founded in 1095 and has in fact been completely rebuilt on several occasions since then. Among the curiosities you can see is an unusual, so-called "Penitent's Pew," in which sinners had to sit and confess their sins aloud to the whole congregation.

In the vaults, wood coffins and mummies can be seen in a remarkably healthy state of preservation. Some of them have been here for more than 200 years; saved from certain deterioration by the dry air prevalent in the rooms of the crypt or perhaps by its high methane content. It's all a bit spooky.

The last imposing official building to be designed by

The limestone vaults of St. Michan's Church preserve bodies buried there.

The Hugh Lane Municipal Gallery offers a Sunday concert series in the spring.

the architect James Gandon was the **King's Inns**, which houses the headquarters of the Irish legal profession. It contains an important law library and a magnificent dining hall, where grand portraits of many judges decorate the walls.

On the north side of Parnell Square is Charlemont House, one of Dublin's most attractive 18th-century mansions, which is now the **Hugh Lane Municipal Gallery of Modern Art** (web site <www.hughlane.ie>). It includes magnificent pieces from the superb collection of Sir Hugh Lane, whose drowning in the *Lusitania* disaster of 1915 provoked a long legal struggle over custody of his paintings. For 20 years his pictures shuttled back and forth between Dublin and London, but the current agreement assures the Municipal Gallery three-quarters of the contested legacy, including works by Corot, Courbet, Manet, Monet, and Rousseau.

Beyond the Center

The **Phoenix Park** provides Dubliners with nearly 3 sq miles (8 sq km) of beautiful parkland. Its huge monument is an obelisk honoring the Duke of Wellington, who was born in Ireland, but was later to quip that although a man may be born in a stable, that wouldn't make him a horse. Among the numerous buildings discreetly located in the park are the residence of the President of Ireland (*Áras an Uachtaráin*), and the Ashtown Castle Heritage Center, which details the history of the park and its flora and fauna. On the northeast side of Phoenix Park, Dublin **zoo** provides education and diversion; it is noted for breeding lion cubs in captivity.

In Kilmainham on the South Circular Road, a stone tower gate guards the grounds of the **Royal Hospital**, which as the city's main 17th-century building, was a home for army pensioners. Now it is the **Irish Museum of Modern Art**.

The ugly and forbidding **Kilmainham Gaol** has been restored as if it were a work of art. The prisoners who lived and died within its walls include many of the heroes of Irish nationalism. The jail is open daily to visitors from April–Sept (during winter months, Mon–Fri 9:30am–5pm). The central cell-block shows exhibits from Ireland's stormy history.

Jails make unlikely tourist attractions, as do factories. Nevertheless, many make their way to the city's biggest enterprise, the **Guinness Brewery** based at St. James' Gate site since 1759. Its dark, full-bodied stout is world-renowned. Visitors are shown a film of the manufacturing process and can sample the finished product. There's also an exhibition space where art shows are sometimes on display.

In the Ballsbridge district of southeast Dublin you can find the spacious grounds of the **Royal Dublin Society** (RDS). A golden and green privet hedge surrounds the fields in which one of the greatest horse shows in the world is held (in August). The RDS complex is also used for agricultural and industrial exhibitions, as well as conferences and concerts.

This area, rich in parkland and large residences, boasts many foreign embassies, a fair number of them in Ailesbury Road. Just around the corner is the **Chester Beatty Library**

and Gallery of Oriental Art. Its collection is well-known for priceless manuscripts and miniatures from the East: jade books from China, early Arabic tomes on geography and astronomy, and a sampling of Korans. The collector and donor behind all this was Sir Alfred Chester Beatty (1875-1968), an American who retired to Ireland.

DUBLIN DAYTRIPS

In the northeastern part of the Bay, **Howth peninsula** makes an appealing starting point for those wishing to venture out of Dublin. From the vantage point of the 170-m (560-ft) Hill of Howth, you can survey the bay and the open sea. Howth Harbor, on the north side of the peninsula, is a fishing port as well as a haven for pleasure boats. From here you can see and visit Ireland's Eye, an islet a mile offshore that is popular with birds and bird-watchers.

Malahide, a small resort town, is perhaps best known for its **castle**, a two-turreted medieval pile with a lived-in look. The spirit of the Talbot family, who resided here for 791 years, still pervades—not only through the portraits on the walls, but even in the color of the walls, "Malahide orange." It is a tint found only here. Part of the National Portrait Collection is also here. Lawns surround the castle, bought by the Dublin County Council after the death of the last Lord Talbot in 1975.

The Fry Model Railway Museum is the largest model railway in Ireland and one of the largest in Europe. It shows transport in Ireland dating back more than 150 years, and all of it is electronically controlled.

Drogheda is an industrial township with a population of 24,000. It straddles the River Boyne near to where the 1690 battle took place in which King James II lost his chance to recover the English crown (see page 19). This medieval city was surrounded by a wall with ten gates—you can still drive through the 13th-century **St. Lawrence's Gate**, with its two towers standing as vigilantly as ever. In the town center **St. Peter's Church** has been dedicated to St. Oliver Plunkett (1628-1681), the Archbishop of Armagh, who was executed by the British in connection with an alleged Popish Plot. Several relics of the local saint are displayed in the church including the actual door of his cell at Newgate Prison and, most amazing of all, his head, which is embalmed and kept in a gold case in a side altar.

About 10 km (6 miles) to the northwest is **Monasterboice** (St. Buite's Abbey), one of the numerous ancient Irish monastic settlements. Above it all stands the jagged top of what is thought to have been the tallest round tower in Ireland, 34 m (110 ft) high. Along with the remains of two ruined churches there are three important examples of early Christian high crosses. Many of the intricately carved figures portray New Testament subjects; others are abstract.

A high medieval gatehouse sternly guards the approach to **Mellifont Abbey**, Ireland's most important early Cistercian monastery. The buildings include the remains of a large church and the Lavabo, which is a most unusual and graceful octagonal building of which only four sides remain today. Like most other abandoned monastic institutions, Mellifont is set in peaceful and verdant country.

Newgrange, a massive Neolithic tomb, looks like a man-made hilltop. It is an amazing feat of prehistoric engineering, and not least because of the narrow tunnel leading to the central shrine, which was positioned to let the sun shine in precisely on the shortest day of the year, 21 December. Newgrange, on the north bank of the Boyne, is considered one of Europe's best examples of a passage-grave. The 19-m (62-ft) tunnel is just about high and wide enough for you to walk through at a crouch. At the end of it you can stand in the circular vault and look up at the ceiling and marvel at the incredible 4,000-year-old technique used in its construction.

Intriguing carvings can be seen in spiral, circular and diamond designs, decorating the stones in the inner sanctum, and at the entrance. Outside, a dozen large, upright stones, about one-third of those originally placed here, form a protective circle around the mound. There is an extensive heritage center at the site. Two further Neolithic tumuli were discovered nearby at two places called Knowth and Dowth, which suggests that this was regarded as a special place in prehistoric times.

The scribes and artists of the monastery at **Kells**, located in County Meath, are credited with producing the nation's most beautiful book, now on display at Trinity College in Dublin (see page 29). The town of Kells has grown up around the monastic settlement, and there is a fine Celtic cross standing at the main traffic intersection. Near the cemetery are several other high stone crosses and a round tower, practically intact and almost 30 m (100 ft) high.

As its name indicates, **Trim** is a well-kept, tidy town. In fact, the terse English name is derived from the Irish *Baile Atha Trium*, which means "the town of the Elder Tree Ford." The river in question is the Boyne, which adds greatly to the beauty of the area.

Trim claims it has Ireland's largest medieval **castle**, once a Norman stronghold. Vast it is, but time has left only the bare bones. The Dublin Gate in the south once contained a prison. On the opposite side of the river, the Yellow Steeple is like a finger pointing upwards. It was part of an Augustinian abbey established in the 13th century; the tower was blown up deliberately to keep it out of the hands of Cromwell.

West of Dublin, landlocked **County Kildare** has some of the greenest pastures in all of Ireland. It's a great area for sports, and there is no shortage of historic sites amidst the rolling hills.

Maynooth, a pleasant town with an historic college and the ruins of a 12th-century castle, is a training school for priests. Founded in 1795, **St. Patrick's College** is seen as one of the foremost Catholic seminaries in the world.

On the edge of the village of Celbridge, **Castletown House** stands at the end of a long avenue of trees. This stately home, in Palladian style, was erected in 1722 for the speaker of the Irish House of Commons, William Conolly, and has been restored and refurnished with 18th-century antiques and paintings.

About 5 km (3 miles) from the house Conolly's widow ordered the construction of a monstrous obelisk. Known as Conolly's Folly, it was erected, with the best of intentions, to provide employment for local workers who were suffering from the Great Famine of 1740.

The administrative center of the county, Naas (the Irish *Nas na Riogh*, means Assembly Place of the Kings), has an important racecourse. So does nearby Punchestown. The capital of horse racing and breeding is the **Curragh**, a prairie from Droichead Nua (New Bridge) all the way to Kildare Town, but it's still a shock to come upon a modern grandstand—site of the Irish Sweeps Derby—right in the middle of this endless plain.

Many of the winners of the world's big races were born at the **National Stud Farm** at Tully. Here the thoroughbreds live in the equivalent of a first-class motel. Visitors are allowed in from Easter to October. Besides the Irish Horse Museum, there is an immaculate **Japanese Garden** adjoining the Stud. At the beginning of the 20th century, one Japanese gardener and 40 local men worked for four long years to transform an Irish bog into a little world of sheared shrubs, disciplined trees, a lotus pond, and even a teahouse and red wooden bridge.

A bridge to tranquility: Visit the Japanese gardens at Ireland's National Stud Farm.

The town of **Kildare** is also remembered for the unusual double monastery (monks and nuns) founded there by the fifth-century St. Brigid. Though the buildings were quite badly damaged by the Vikings and many other invaders, the shape of the 19th-century **cathedral** (Church of Ireland) features 13th-century elements. Nearby you can also inspect an ancient round tower still in very good shape, with stairs all the way to the summit.

The ruins of another ancient monastery are at the southern end of County Kildare, in the village of **Castledermot**. Only two beautifully carved crosses remain, and the portal of a church that could be as much as a thousand years old. The design of this ruin has been repeated in a new church just a few yards behind it.

Dún Laoghaire, just south of Dublin, is Ireland's leading yachting center. The piers at the harbor are 2 km (1 mile) long, leaving plenty of space between for the huge fleet of pleasure boats that dock here, as well as the car ferry terminal. Construction of the harbor was seen as a great feat of 19th-century marine engineering—and it's still impressive. You can also visit the Maritime Museum, which features many exhibits relating to Ireland's maritime history. Dún Laoghaire, Dublin's largest suburb, is pronounced "Dunleary."

About a mile to the south at **Sandycove** is an 18th-century tower. James Joyce lived in it, and used this experience in the opening of his work *Ulysses*. The Martello Tower (named after a Corsican headland with a fort) was part of a network of coastal defenses built to ward off an invasion by Napoleon, and has now been turned into a museum dedicated to Joyce. A second Martello Tower can be seen on Dalkey Island, the largest of a group of islands off Dalkey.

Just across the border in County Wicklow, the popular resort of **Bray** has a 2-km (1-mile) sand-and-shingle beach backed by an esplanade. The Wicklow coast is mostly sandy and low-lying, and the interior of the county is known as the Garden of Ireland.

West of Bray, near the small village of Enniskerry, is the most majestic park you're ever likely to see. The grand estate of **Powerscourt** descends in disciplined terraces to a lake with a fountain in the middle. Taking in manifold acres of elegant, spectacular scenery, it has an 18th-century, 100-room mansion at its center, which was unfortunately damaged in a fire in 1974. The house and grounds are open to the public daily except for two weeks prior to Christmas (web site <www.powerscourt.ie>). There is a new garden center that is also worth a visit. The Powerscourt Waterfall, 5 km (3 miles) south of the house itself, may be visited all year round.

In the ruins of the ancient monastic city of **Glendalough** tombstones dating back hundreds of years alternate with more newly covered graves. The original gateway to the settlement is still standing, the only one of its kind remaining in Ireland. Inside, on the right, a cross-inscribed stone may have marked the limit of the sanctuary granted to all those who took refuge within the monastery.

As you enter this site, which is located in a narrow, wooded valley, you suddenly stumble across the perfectly preserved historic **round tower**, a thousand years old. With its graceful, tapered shape and pert conical roof, it might easily be mistaken for a missile on a launch pad. This tower was the place to sit out any sieges; its doorway is built 3.5 m (11½ ft) above the ground—enough to discourage even Vikings from attempting an invasion.

The hermit St. Kevin founded the monastery in the sixth century. Inspired by the breathtaking scenery and the remoteness of the locale, he planned it as the site of a small, contemplative institution. As its fame spread far and wide, Glendalough of the Seven Churches became an important monastic city, until 1398, when it was destroyed by Anglo-Normans. The ruins

Stroll through the extraordinary gardens of Powerscourt Estate.

of the churches and buildings are particularly evocative, set as they are amid wild beauty.

In **Avondale**, you can visit the home of Charles Stewart Parnell, the great 19th century Irish leader, which has been restored in 1850s style. It is set in an area of verdant forest and woodland and makes an ideal destination for walkers. Grand **Russborough House**, near Blessington, is an 18th-century house in grand Palladian style. Today it houses the Sir Alfred Beit art collection, and is beautifully and richly decorated, offering magnificent views across the ornamental lake toward the splendid Wicklow mountains.

THE SOUTHEAST

Meteorologists confirm what everyone in Ireland has always believed: on average, over the whole year, the southeast enjoys up to an hour more sunshine a day than other parts of Ireland. The better to see—and enjoy—the varied scenery, mountains and pastures, rivers, beautiful beaches, and delightful old towns.

Enniscorthy (the Irish *Inis Coirthe* means Rock Island) is a colorful inland port on the River Slaney, navigable from here to Wexford. High above the steep streets of the town, Vinegar Hill is a good vantage point for viewing the countryside. It was the scene of the last battle of the 1798 Rising, during which British General Lake overwhelmed the many Wexford rebels armed with pitchforks and pikes, dashing the struggle for independence.

Enniscorthy Castle, set in the center of town, is a Norman keep which was rebuilt during the 16th century and was recently opened as a folk museum.

Wexford, the county seat, (24km/15 miles to the south) lays claim to a most historic past, having been one of the first Viking settlements in the land. In the ninth century it was called *Waesfjord*, meaning "the harbor of the mudflats." At low tide the original name still seems appropriate.

A few ancient monuments survive and are well signposted, with informative plaques explaining almost every legend of Wexford, which only adds to the interest of strolling around the back streets. All the remaining medieval walls have now been fully restored and a heritage center has opened.

In addition, you can visit the **Irish National Heritage Park** in Ferrycarrig, north of town, to see a collection of life-size replicas of ancient dwellings, burial sites, old monastic settlements and various types of fortification, from early Irish man up to the 12th century. Reminders of the area's seafaring past are on view at the Maritime Museum in the little, picturesque village of Kilmore Quay, about 25 km (15 miles) south of Wexford. Housed in an old lightship, moored permanently in the harbor, the museum has numerous maritime artifacts to examine.

In the month of October, the Wexford Opera Festival offers a magnetic attraction for world performers and fans for even little-known works. The town is very proud of its year-round cultural pursuits.

Southeast of the town, the resort of **Rosslare** has a sight for sore eyes: a 10-km (6-mile) crescent of beach. Beyond it is Rosslare Harbor, where car ferries arrive from and depart for Fishguard, Le Havre, and Cherbourg.

Continuing this theme and just before turning inland, the tip of the **Hook peninsula** has a tall, 700-year-old lighthouse that warns mariners of the treacherous rocks, and signals the entrance to the Waterford harbor. But that's only half the story; a light has been kept burning at Hook Head for the last 1,500 years.

The Norse established ports such as Dublin and Wexford, but it somehow never occurred to them to found permanent settlements inland. It was the Normans who moved 32 km

Roll along the river—a cyclist takes advantage of the path beside River Slaney in Enniscorthy, County Wexford.

(20 miles) up the estuary to build the town of **New Ross**, still an important inland port. In the middle of the 13th century, it was encircled by a strong and defensive wall.

The small, isolated hamlet of **Dunganstown**, near New Ross, was the birthplace of the great grandfather of President John F. Kennedy. A plaque marks the cottage from which he emigrated to Boston.

The assassinated president was much admired in Ireland, and you can often see his picture hanging like an icon on living-room walls. A group of Irish-Americans and the Irish government later created the **John F. Kennedy Park**, above Dunganstown. This appealing green memorial contains both mighty oak and chestnut trees, as well as shrubs, flowers, and trimmed lawns. Visitors can follow the signposted walks or relax with a picnic.

Heading southwest, over to County Waterford, you cross the historic frontier between the provinces of Leinster and

Munster. As the largest in area of Ireland's four provinces, Munster boasts the cities of Cork and Limerick as well as thinly inhabited farmland and romantic Atlantic shores.

With a population of 95,000, **Waterford** is a busy little port situated just 29 km (18 miles) from the open sea. From the far side of the River Suir, its long quayside presents a pretty European image. Waterford's foundation can be traced back to the ninth century, but it did not gain its first charter until 1205, granted by King John of Magna Carta fame. The heritage center in town has many ancient relics from the Norse and Norman settlements of the city, and numerous municipal mementos are preserved inside **Reginald's Tower**, the city's most venerable building.

The walls of this massive circular fortification, 3 m (10 ft) thick and about 24 m (80 ft) tall, have survived many sieges since they went up in 1003, and the tower has had a checkered past, serving as a fortress, an arsenal, and a mint, as well as a barracks and prison. Now it contains the Waterford Civic Museum.

Among other attractions are the Garter Lane Arts Center, perhaps the country's leading regional center of its kind. Old mill buildings on the quays house an extensive heritage center, complementing the existing one at Reginald's Tower. The center offers a detailed overview of Waterford's history over 1,500 years, focusing on the port's industrial past. There are also restaurants and craft shops.

An elegant Georgian street, the Mall, begins at the Quay. Waterford City Hall, built during the 1780s, has many distinguished features, including two small theaters and a Council Chamber elegantly and brightly illuminated by a splendid chandelier—made, logically, from the famous Waterford glass.

The golden age of **Waterford glass** ran from 1783 to 1851. After a century's lapse, production was resumed, and the traditional processes can still be seen on guided tours of the factory, about 5 km (3 miles) from Waterford town center on the Cork road. It's best to check with the local tourist office before making a visit.

At the western edge of the county, you can sample the Lismore Experience, another educational multimedia show. It tells the history of this small town, which was founded in the seventh century by St. Carthage. Also, visit Ormond Castle in Carrick-on-Suir. This is a fine example of an old Elizabethan manor, now restored to its 16th century glory.

Reginald's Tower has served as an arsenal, a mint, a barracks, even a prison.

Castles and Kings

The counties of **Kilkenny** and **Tipperary** both feature stunning river valleys and imposing ruins from a regal past. Tipperary was once used as the home of the kings of Munster; Kilkenny has its own glory; it entered history as the ancient Kingdom of Ossory.

The main town in County Tipperary is called **Clonmel**. A hamlet probably existed here before the Vikings. The town was walled in the 14th century, and parts of this can still be seen. The turreted West Gate was rebuilt in 1831 on the site of an original town gate. The county museum in Parnell Street is well worth a visit.

The name of the township of **Cahir** is a short version of the Irish for "Fortress of the Dun Abounding in Fish." Its setting, on the River Suir, is both fetching and strategic.

Upstream from the bridge, a family of swans bob above the weir; downstream a seemingly impregnable castle guards the crucial crossing. Built on the river's lovely islet—a site that has been fortified since the third century—the present castle may date from the 15th century, or possibly earlier; the records are vague. It's in a fine state of restoration now and so is well worth a visit. Guided tours point out many military details, such as musket slits, a portcullis, and a cannonball embedded high in one of the walls. While you're in Cahir, take a look at **Swiss Cottage**, an early 19th-century cottage ornée, in the bright style of the former Brighton Pavilion. It has been fully restored right down to the thatched roof and original French wallpaper.

In **Cashel** (County Tipperary), ruins majestically crown an imposing hilltop. On the **Rock of Cashel**, a 61-m- (200-ft-) high outcrop of limestone in the middle of a pasture, the

Not like the others—Cormac's Chapel was built by Irish monks interpreting various European architectural styles.

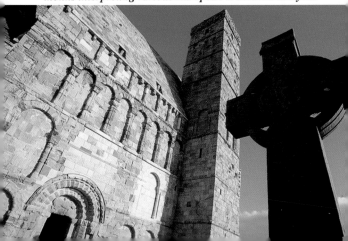

kings of Munster established their headquarters from the fourth to the 12th century. When St. Patrick visited in 450, he baptized King Aengus and his brothers. The hill was handed in 1101 to the ecclesiastical authorities, who built an Irish-Romanesque church on it.

Cormac's Chapel (consecrated in 1134) is different from all of the others because it was built by Irish monks who interpreted the different architectural styles they had studied in Europe. It features a steeply pitched stone roof, rows of blank arches, and two strangely positioned towers. Stone-carvings of beasts and abstract designs decorate the doorway and arches.

The chapel is dwarfed by the **cathedral** which abuts it. This structure, dating from the 13th century, has both thick and well-preserved walls, but the roof collapsed during the 18th century. On the positive side, the resulting hole lets the sunlight stream in, helping to clarify the many architectural details, as well as the exquisite medieval stone-carvings.

St. Patrick's Cross, inside the entrance, is one of the oldest crosses in Ireland, and it looks like it—the sculptures on both sides are very weatherbeaten. Interestingly the cross rises up from the "Coronation Stone," said to have been a sacrificial altar in pagan times.

With all these incomparable structures featured below, the perfect round tower looming above seems somehow to be a bit of an anticlimax.

It was in the lively market town of **Thurles**, in 1174, that the Irish forces defeated the Anglo-Norman army led by Strongbow (see page 17). Seven hundred years later, the town was to be the birthplace of the Gaelic Athletic Association (GAA), now an amateur sports organization. The GAA center offers a multimedia show on the history of Gaelic games.

The 13th-century Kilkenny Castle, once held by the Butler family and now owned by the state, is rich in Irish history.

The most conspicuous landmark of the town, the Catholic Cathedral, is a 19th-century impression of the Romanesque style. The square bell tower, 38 m (125 ft) high, can be seen for miles around.

Six km (four miles) south of Thurles, on the west bank of the River Suir, **Holy Cross Abbey** boasts a 12th-century church which is still in daily use. The name of the church refers to a particle of the True Cross, enshrined in this old Cistercian Abbey over several centuries.

Construction of the church was started in Romanesque style, but the rebuilding and expansion programs over the next centuries evolved into Gothic. The solid white walls, enhanced by window-tracery, reach up to a perfectly restored

15th-century ceiling. Experts acclaim the beautiful sedilia, and the triple-arched recess containing seats of honor carved from jet-black marble and decorated with ancient coats of arms. Another detail is the night stairs, down which the monks stumbled from their sleeping quarters at 2am to chant matins. One of the bells in the tower was cast in the early 13th century, making it Ireland's oldest.

Kilkenny has a colorful past and present. Among other surprises, you will find, smack in the traffic-clogged city center, an enormous medieval castle with acres of lawns—and a river to boot. This was the capital of the old Kingdom of Ossory, a small, feuding realm in pre-Norman Ireland.

Parliament, which convened here in 1366, passed the notorious but ineffectual Statute of Kilkenny with the aim of segregating the Irish from the Anglo-Normans; in those days intermarriage was seen as high treason. In the 17th century an independent Irish parliament met here for several years. Cromwell took the town in 1650, suffering heavy losses in the process but in the end capturing it.

The Irish *Cill Choinnigh* means St. Canice's church. **St. Canice's Cathedral**, built in the 13th century, is on the original site of the church, which gave the town its name. Though Cromwell's rampaging troops badly damaged the building, it has since been restored to an admirable state. Medieval sculptures and monuments abound in this Protestant church. Alongside it is a round tower, part of the ancient church, so tall, slim, and austere that it resembles a factory smokestack.

Kilkenny Castle was built in the 13th century to replace the original primitive fortress erected by Strongbow. The Butler family, one of the great Anglo-Norman dynasties, held the castle until 1935, but today it is owned by the Irish state. Three of the castle's original four towers remain. You will also

Jerpoint Abbey contains monuments to knights, saints, and sculptors alike.

find a brilliantly restored picture gallery on the upper floor of the north wing.

Kilkenny (with a population of 75,000) is packed with bright shops. In the High Street, the Tholsel, dating from the 18th century, has an eight-sided clock tower like a lighthouse. The Archaeological Society in Kilkenny runs a museum in **Rothe House**, a Tudor town house dating to 1594. The exhibits on display range from Stone Age tools unearthed locally to medieval relics.

Not far from Thomastown (in County Kilkenny) you can visit the partially restored ruins of **Jerpoint Abbey**, an ancient Cistercian monastery. Founded in the middle of the 12th century by the King of Ossory, it had a relatively brief and very troubled history involving several rivalries with neighboring institutions, government pressures to keep out Irish monks, and, finally, the dissolution of the monasteries during the year 1540.

Parts of the church retain the Romanesque lines, but the square central tower with its stepped battlements was added during the 15th century. Much of the sculptural work in the half-restored cloister and the church itself is intact, and you can see larger than life carvings of knights and saintly figures, which make inspiring monuments not only to those they honor, but also to the many talented sculptors who worked devotedly at this abbey in the Middle Ages.

THE SOUTHWEST

County Cork

Ireland's largest county (the farthest south) marries gently rolling farmland with rugged, stony peninsulas and visually delightful bays. Here you will find the people are witty and chatty; after all, this is the home of the blarney.

Cork City (population 130,000) enjoys all the usual facilities—and traffic jams—of an important commercial and industrial center, but its atmosphere is entirely unique. This is perhaps because of the River Lee, about which the poet Edmund Spenser wrote:

The spreading Lee, that like an island fayre
Encloseth Cork with his divided flood ...

The dark green waterway that attracts hungry seagulls, elegant white swans, and giant freighters to the center of town accounts for a good deal of the atmospheric mood. So do the steep hills enclosing the urban valleys and the many historic landmarks to be found in the area, of which Corkonians are proud and sentimental.

Incidentally, just to dispel some myths: The name of the city has nothing to do with trees or bottle-stoppers. Cork, an anglicization of *Corcaigh*, is unpromisingly translated as "Marshy Place," which is how the area looked back in the sixth century when St. Finbarr arrived to found a church and school. In the year 820 the Vikings raided marshy Cork, destroying the institutions and houses, but they liked the lay of the land and so returned to build their own town on the same site. This destruction and rebuilding was repeated like a pattern in the 17th century and then again during the "Troubles" of 1919–1921.

Seeing any city on foot is an opportunity to take a closer look at its monuments and people. The main office for Cork

Cork City: A sea of neighboring rooftops, as glimpsed from the roof of St. Anne's Church.

and Kerry Tourism is located on the Grand Parade in Cork. They offer free maps of the city centre highlighting the its many attraction's. Cork's beauty begs slow exploration and one can easily spend the day strolling along its narrow canals and winding streets. Some highlights are:

Red Abbey is the last remaining vestige of the medieval monasteries in Cork. It is said that in 1690 the Duke of Marlborough witnessed the siege of the city from its tower, his artillery being fired at the town walls from the garden down below.

Patrick Street. The wide main street of Cork is curved because it was built above a river channel. It offers great window-shopping and people promenading; throngs appear on Saturday afternoons.

St. Finbarr's Cathedral (Church of Ireland). The latest version, built in the 19th century, follows the lofty French-Gothic style, with arches upon arches.

Shandon Church. This pepper-pot belfry has always been a favorite city landmark. Visitors can climb up through the clockwork intricacies and even play a tune on the bells.

Heritage Park, Blackrock. Offers cameos of Cork life and the history of the Cork fire brigade; the only such fire service museum in Ireland.

Cork City Gaol, Sunday's Well. The cells of the prison have been fully restored to the 19th/early 20th-century style. The gaol also houses the national broadcasting museum.

Cork City's many **quaysides** give a fascinating view of the river, bridges and boats, the skyline, and the hills beyond.

Cork is a good center for excursions. **Blarney Castle,** 8 km (5 miles) to the north, became world famous when Queen Elizabeth I made it a common noun. The owner of the castle, Cormac MacCarthy by family name, and Baron of Blarney, incurred the queen's displeasure by his constant delaying tactics and soothing but evasive chatter. "It's the usual blarney," the queen is supposed to have said. Today, tourists climb up to the battlement, lie flat on their backs, hang on to two iron bars, and extend the head down backwards to kiss the awkwardly placed stone.

The castle itself is worth a visit, even if mighty hordes of tourists do besiege it every summer. The formidable keep was built in the middle of the 15th century, while the private park, in which the castle stands, includes a cool, slightly mysterious dell with ancient occult connections.

In ports around the world, ships are seen with *Cobh* on the stern. You may have wondered how to pronounce it. **Cobh**, Ireland's biggest south coast seaport, lies about 24 km (15 miles) east of Cork City, and pronounced "Cove," which is also exactly what it means in Irish.

From Queen Victoria's visit in 1849, until 1922, Cobh was called Queenstown. The port is touched by nostalgia—from

All to the glory of God—the Cathedral of St. Colman houses a 47-bell carillon amidst its grand Gothic arches.

the days of the great transatlantic liners and the earlier, more tragic traffic of desperate emigrants fleeing the Irish famine for Canada or America. The Queenstown Experience provides a particular insight into this era. The Cunard shipping office is now a bank. High above the harbor, the spire of the **Cathedral of St. Colman** reaches heavenward. Recitals are given in the summer on the cathedral's 47-bell carillon.

If you're in Midleton, visit the Jameson Heritage Center in a converted whiskey distillery that dates back to the late 18th century. It tells the story of Irish whiskey via an audio-visual presentation, and offers a tour with tastings.

The town of **Youghal** (in English pronounced "Yawl") is a resort with 8 km (5 miles) of beach and a long seafaring history. It is renowned for its fine lace, *point d'Irlande*. The town walls from the Middle Ages can still be seen.

On the site of the main town gate is the **clock tower** from 1776. The main street runs right through it with the structure's four narrow floors and belfry rising above an arched platform over the street. The tower is an attractive landmark—except for its past. It was once the prison, and insurrectionists were hanged from the windows to set an example to the populace.

The most impressive monument, **St. Mary's Collegiate Church** (Church of Ireland), is thought to have been founded in the fifth century. Most of the present structure went up in the 13th century, with detailed restoration in the 19th. Among the monuments and tombs in the church is one built, in his own honor, by Richard Boyle, a wheeler-dealer of the Elizabethan age and the first Earl of Cork. Myrtle Grove, a superb 16th-century house near the churchyard entrance, was the home of Sir Walter Raleigh, once the mayor of Youghal. The heritage museum on the quayside gives an excellent account of the town's history.

Steep green hills shelter the seaport of **Kinsale**, about 29 km (18 miles) south of Cork. As its big harbor is virtually landlocked, it is a joy to sailors and sightseers alike. For a community of less than 2,000 people, Kinsale is renowned for its restaurants, among the best in southwest Ireland.

This was the scene of the siege of 1601 in which the Spanish troops sailed to the aid of the Irish against Queen Elizabeth and took over the town, but were defeated, sparking the "flight of the Earls," the exodus of the Irish nobility and the redistribution of their lands. Kinsale became a British naval base.

Today, the picturesque **harbor** is used by fishing boats, sailing dinghies and yachts. Ashore, there are **fortifications** to explore, the Norman church of St. Multose, a small castle where prisoners-of-war were held, a museum containing the first town charter of Edward III, and the **Desmond Castle and Wine Museum**.

Large colonies of breeding and migratory birds inhabit the **Old Head** of Kinsale, 16 km (10 miles) beyond the town. A modern lighthouse here is the successor to a beacon dating back to pre-Christian times. It was off the Old Head that a German submarine torpedoed the world-famous liner, the *Lusitania,* on 7 May 1915, resulting in the loss of 1,500 lives. The inquest into the horrendous disaster was held in the Kinsale Court House.

En route from Kinsale to Bantry, Clonakilty's **West Cork Model Railway Village** depicts the area's six towns, complete with a working model of the defunct West Cork Railway.

In West Cork, the town of **Bantry** nestles between steep green hills and a bay that looks like a lake. Whiddy Island, at the head of the bay, was an oil storage depot—until a tanker accident some years ago.

The main sight in Bantry itself is Bantry House, a part-Georgian and Victorian stately home set in tropical gardens. The tapestries, paintings and furnishing can be viewed on weekdays year round, and the house also offers an Armada Center, in which an ill-fated attempt by the French to land in Bantry Bay in 1796 is recreated.

Heading counter-clockwise around the bay from Bantry, the highway weaves through progressively more rocky hills until it descends upon **Glengarriff**, where the beauty of the setting and the Mediterranean climate account for its year-round popularity.

Ferryboats will take you round the bay from Glengarriff to **Garinish Island**, a 15-hectare (37-acre) eden run by the Office of Public Works. The flora comes from a total of five continents, and the centerpiece of all the horticultural achievement is a stunning walled **Italian garden**, surrounding a pool, with the gentle air of a divine and paradisiacal perfume factory. In the 19th century Garinish was a bleak military outpost. You can climb to the top of the Martello tower, where sentries once kept a lookout for Napoleonic invasion fleets, and survey the luxuriant hills around the bay.

County Kerry

By any standard this is a spectacular part of the world: the Atlantic in all its moods, lakes designed for lovers or poets, and steep, evergreen mountains. The people, who live in this, the Kingdom of Kerry, are special too—gregarious, outgoing, and most generous.

When in Bantry... visit the Bantry House, with interiors as lush as its tropical gardens.

Killarney, the center of the lakes district, can provide anything a visitor may need, from housing and food to fishing tackle. Seeing the sights here can be accomplished in many ways—by car, coach, bicycle, boat, or even by "jaunting car," a horse-drawn rig driven by a *jarvey* (guide) who knows the territory and how to tell a story on the way.

Near Killarney

Due to the difficult terrain and logistical problems, it is best to visit the **Gap of Dunloe** and **Lakes of Killarney** on a fully organized excursion, usually an all-day trip. The gap, a wild gorge 6 km (4 miles) long, can be traversed by pony-back, in a pony trap, or, if you insist, on foot. Sound effects underline the weirdness of the eerie rock-strewn scenery as echoes bounce off the mountains — **MacGillycuddy's Reeks** in the west (the highest range in Ireland), and to the east, **Purple Mountain**. The long trek leads to the shore of the Upper Lake, where the tour continues by boat. The scenery around the lakes — thick forests, stark crags and enchanted islands — could not be more romantic, but there's adventure, too: the **rapids** at Old Weir Bridge.

Muckross Abbey is a friary dating from the 15th century with a massive square tower, a cloister with Gothic arches on two sides, Norman or Romanesque on the others, and an old, weathered yew tree. Muckross House, nowadays a museum of Kerry crafts and folklore, is surrounded by outstanding gardens. It is also a traditional farm, with old-style buildings and varied animals, including Kerry cows, native to the county.

The 14th-century ruins of **Ross Castle** are set near old copper mines on a peninsula of the Lower Lake. The castle's garrison surrendered to Oliver Cromwell in 1652, awed by the superstition that strange ships spelled doom. The attackers knew the legend and took advantage by bringing armed vessels from Kinsale.

The **Ring of Kerry** may well be the most sensational 180 km (112 miles) you have ever driven. Set aside a whole day for the circuit so you have enough time to linger over the sublime

Rapids at Old Weir Bridge — among many wondrous sites around Killarney.

sights. The ring is a circular route through hills as steep and round as volcanoes on the way to a coast of rugged cliffs and the most enthralling seascapes. This round-trip can be made in either direction, but here we proceed clockwise.

Leaving Killarney, the road goes past an area of lush lakeland. The first town on the route, **Kenmare**, is famous for lacemaking and the fish which fill its estuary. North of the small resort of Castlecove, a couple of miles off the main road, are the ruins of **Staigue Fort**. A 2,500-year-old stronghold and one of Ireland's main archaeological wonders, this is an almost circular structure about 27 m (90 ft) across with a wall measuring 6 m (18 ft). It predates the invention of cement, so its building and survival was quite a feat.

Near Caherdaniel, the home of Daniel O'Connell ("the Liberator"), has been fully restored and is now a museum. Game fishing is one of the lures for visitors to Waterville, as well as the scenery nearby: pitiless granite mountains on one side of the road, green fields and the sea on the other.

A bridge connects **Valentia Island**, with its high cliffs and vegetation, to the mainland at Portmagee. The island was the

---

Shamrock Curtain

Traveling in the west of Ireland you may suddenly cross the Shamrock Curtain, an invisible cultural frontier. The signs are printed in hard-to-decipher Gaelic letters and the people talk in a cryptic ancient tongue. This means you've stumbled into the Gaeltacht, pockets of green scattered over seven counties. They make up the main line of resistance to the predominance of that mighty international language, English. The Dublin government actively supports the Gaeltacht efforts to keep the old language and culture alive.

Courses in Irish are offered in the **Gaeltacht** every summer. If you can't attend any, don't be afraid to go into the area —it's quite rare to find anyone who can't also speak English.

European terminus of the first Atlantic cable (1866), making possible the first telegraphic contact with America.

Off Valentia, the Skelligs Rocks rise abruptly from the ocean, shrouded with mystery and birds—20,000 pairs of gannets alone. Take a trip to the Skelligs Heritage Center or tour the islands in a boat. The crag caves located on Castleisland are recent rivals to the Aillwee Cave in the Burren and, also impressive—they are nearly 4 km (2½ miles) long.

On the north shore of the peninsula, green hills plunge to sealevel and cliffs complete the descent. **Dingle Bay** seems startlingly wide and the Dingle Peninsula looks almost like another country.

From Glenbeigh to Killorglin, the head of the bay is almost totally protected from the rough sea by huge sandbars extending from either shore. **Rossbeigh Strand**, with its 6 km (4 miles) of golden sand, is a dream beach.

The last town on the ring, **Killorglin**, saves all its energy for three days in August and a mad pagan pageant called the Puck Fair, during which time a mountain goat presides over round-the-clock festivities.

To the north, **Tralee**, with a population of 17,000, the administrative center of County Kerry, owes its fame to the songwriter William Mulchinock (1820-1864). *The Rose of Tralee* and its author are honored in a monument in the town park. The rose also calls the tune of Tralee's annual festival in late August, when girls of Irish descent from many countries compete in a beauty contest, and the winner is crowned Rose of Tralee.

Kerry the Kingdom offers three experiences all in one. Kerry in Color is an audiovisual presentation of the splendors of Kerry; the County Museum gives details of Kerry history since 5000 B.C.; and the Geraldine Experience reconstructs life in medieval Tralee. A steam railway, with a locomotive from the old Tralee-Dingle railway, links the town with the restored, early 19th-century windmill at Blennerville, 3 km (2 miles) away.

Apart from these popular attractions, Tralee is the gateway to the Dingle peninsula, a long, dramatic finger which points some 48 km (30 miles) into the Atlantic. On the south shore, amidst severe cliffs and rocky coves, a sandbar grows into an arc of beach jutting more than halfway across the bay. **Inch Strand's** 6 km (4 miles) of sand slide gently into the sea. Behind the bathers and suntanners, archaeologists putter about the dunes, where inhabitants of prehistoric ages left meaningful debris.

The small fishing port and resort of **Dingle** claims to be the single most westerly town in Europe. From here to land's end all the hamlets are Irish-speaking parts of the Gaeltacht

The craggy Dunmore Head of the Dingle Peninusula—a long, dramatic finger pointing into the Atlantic.

(see page 65), where folklore and traditional language are still thoughtfully preserved.

This is very harsh farming country, where the old stone walls are overrun with shrubs, and hardy vines divide skimpy parcels of land. You'll see the sheep grazing on even the precipitous fields. They usually have splotches of red or blue dye daubed on their backs to affirm ownership and provide a means of telling the different flocks apart.

The western part of the peninsula is very rich territory for archaeologists. In one area, the Fahan group alone consists of a staggering 400 *clocháns* (beehive-shaped stone huts), along with forts, and other ancient structures.

For a spectacular panorama, drive up the **Connor Pass** (at an altitude of 457 m/1,500 ft) and see the sea to the north and south, and mountains and lakes to the east and west. The near-sighted—or fog-bound—can simply admire the wild fuchsia and heather beside the road.

THE WEST

Limerick

By the time the waters of the River Shannon have reached Limerick (population 52,000) in the west, they have flowed over 274 km (170 miles) through thick and thin, from narrow streams and howling rapids to lakes and efficient locks. After Limerick, an important seaport and industrial center, they still have another 97 km (60 miles) to travel through the Shannon estuary to the open Atlantic.

This major position at the meeting of the river and its tidal waters assured the city a long and often violent history. The Danes were first on the scene. Their belligerent policy provoked repeated attacks by the neighboring native Irish, who finally drove them out.

The River Shannon

Briefly deviating from our general progress around the coast, here's an inland foray down the River Shannon. If you don't have the inclination to hire a boat, you can also visit the attractions along the Shannon by car or bus.

Most boat rental is done at Carrick-on-Shannon, the "capital" of County Leitrim, which boasts the superb Costello Chapel of Main Street.

Downstream from Carrick, the river runs into Lough Corry, the first of many interconnected lakes in the Shannon basin. **Lough Ree**, halfway down, is 26 km (16 miles) long and 11 km (7 miles) wide in places, with deserted wooded islands.

The main cross-country roads ford the Shannon at the central market town of **Athlone** with a medieval castle, overlooking the Shannon Bridge. The town has a number of festivals and cultural events (web site <www.athlonechamber.ie>).

At a bend in the river is **Clonmacnois**, an ancient monastic settlement founded in the sixth century by St. Ciaran, which became a major medieval university. Nearby you can follow a 9-km (5½-mile) trip along the Clonmacnois & West Offaly Railway.

Just 6 km (4 miles) south of Clonmacnois, a 16-arch bridge marks Shannonbridge, and at Shannon Harbor the Grand Canal from Dublin meets the river. Portumna is a fishing and boating resort with a new marina.

Lough Derg is the largest of the Shannon lakes—40 km (25 miles) long and up to 5 km (3 miles) wide with islets and fair green hills beyond—a perfect end to the trip.

This is just as well because dangerous rapids abound below **Killaloe**, a prudent place to abandon ship. Killaloe was once a great ecclesiastical center, where **St. Flannan's Cathedral** (Church of Ireland) has been restored to its 12th-century glory. The richly-carved Romanesque doorway is said to be the entrance to the tomb of King Murtagh O'Brien of Munster (d. 1120). The granite shaft nearby, from about the year 1000, bears a bilingual inscription in Runic and Ogham letters—a foretaste of today's Irish-English road signs.

69

King John's Castle once helped Normans defend the River Shannon, now its towers provide fabulous views for tourists.

The Anglo-Normans in turn captured the place with the unpretentious name of *Luimneach*—in English "Bare Spot." King John visited Limerick in 1210 and ordered the construction of a **bridge** and **castle**, which still survive and which have been extensively renovated, However, most of the town walls, behind which the townsfolk gathered during times of siege, were pulled down in the 18th century to make way for civic expansion.

The most memorable siege was endured after the Battle of the Boyne (1690), when the Irish supporters of James II (see page 19) retired to Limerick pursued by William of Orange. In spite of heroic efforts, the losers eventually lost again.

The Treaty of Limerick, which allowed the garrison to leave with honor, softened the blow by guaranteeing the Irish people freedom of religion. But this was repudiated by the then English Parliament and so today Limerick carries the title of "City of the Violated Treaty."

Limerick's major historical monument, the 800-year-old **St. Mary's Cathedral** (Church of Ireland), spans many eras of architecture and art. The great square tower complements the arched Irish-Romanesque west door, while 15th-century carved misericords under the choir seats show free-ranging imagination with representations of an angel, animals such as an eagle, a goat, a dragon, and other figures in relief. The cathedral grounds form the background for a colorful historical audiovisual show with sound and lights.

St. John's Cathedral, which is Catholic, was constructed in Neo-Gothic style, and claims to have the highest spire in Ireland (85 m/280 ft). Next to the cathedral, reconstruction and restoration work on a grand scale is reviving St. John's Square, an elegant 18th-century urban ensemble.

The 18th-century waterfront Custom House is being fully restored to house the priceless Hunt collection of antiquities and *objets d'art*, currently kept by the University of Limerick. The word "limerick" comes from the merry refrain "Will you come up to Limerick?", part of an old parlor game, in which the participants had to make up a nonsense verse.

Shannon Airport reinforces Limerick's historic role as a center of commerce. It opened in 1945, making its mark before fast and non-stop transatlantic travel became the

St. Mary's Cathedral is Limerick's foremost historical monument.

order of the day. Passengers who were waiting for their planes to be refuelled were offered a diversion—the chance to buy luxury goods exempt from tax. Thus the world's first duty-free shop grew into a shopping center, and the airport became the hub of an industrial development with tax concessions.

The Shannon Free Airport Development Company then took over the management of **Bunratty Castle**, and turned it into a busy tourist attraction. The castle, about 5 km (3 miles) from the airport, has been restored. At night "Medieval Banquets" are recreated for visitors by professional Irish entertainers in period costumes accompanied by traditional music from the Irish harp.

A favorite attraction of the Bunratty tourist complex is a **Folk Park** containing replicas of typical old houses of the Shannon region. The peat fires are kept burning, as if the people had just stepped out to milk a cow or catch a fish.

A new marina has been built in **Kilrush**, where the heritage center details the history of the town and Scattery, a nearby island and Christian settlement. At Foynes, you can visit the flying boat museum, which has old newsreels among its many attractions.

The administrative center of County Clare, **Ennis** has a 13th-century friary, which in the Middle Ages had 350 friars and, amazingly, 600 students. The buildings were expanded and re-vamped over the years, and finally fully renovated in the 1950s.

☛ The Burren

North west of Ennis, more than 518sq km (200 square miles) of County Clare belongs to **the Burren**—a set of geological formations. Glaciers and the erosion of ages have created limestone "pavements"—horizontal slabs divided by fissures, like the aftermath of an earthquake.

Though it is sometimes described as a moonscape, the Burren is anything but barren; it is a quiet world of small animals, birds, butterflies, and Mediterranean flowers. It may seem hostile to human habitation, but the profusion of forts and tombs proves that it supported a population for several centuries.

Geologists, botanists and archaeologists have field trips on the "pavements," and speleologists enjoy checking out the caves. More than 40 km (25 miles) of caves have been fully explored. Most of them are for experts only, but anyone can visit Aillwee Cave, southeast of Ballyvaughan (open April to October). In Kilfenora, a village on the edge of this plain, citizens have established the original **Burren Display Center**, as a quick and pleasant way to get your bearings. Kilfenora Cathedral, dating from about the 12th century, is noted for its sculptured monuments, and the village has many high crosses.

The **Cliffs of Moher**, just 6 miles (10 km) north west of Lahinch, tower 213 m (700 ft) over the Atlantic Ocean. From O'Brien's Tower, an outpost near to the edge, the spectacle moves the spirit: The cliff-faces stand above the sea posing for pictures, the horizontal layers are as easily defined with the eye as the storeys of a glass skyscraper. You watch a great wave crash against the foot of the cliff but the thump is heard a little late, like the report of a distant artillery shell. Many thousands of seabirds live on the cliffs.

The town of **Lisdoonvarna** is famous as a spa and has its own atmosphere of romance. The springs produce waters which are rich in numerous minerals, including sulphur, iron, and iodine, thought to be good for rheumatic conditions and as a general tonic.

Though not very romantic in itself, the town has gained a reputation as a matchmaking mecca, and indeed people from all over the country have arrived in Lisdoonvarna in an attempt to find a mate, making Ireland's first spa their last resort. More recently folk music festivals have broadened the appeal, and also lowered the average age at local dances.

The cliffs of Moher rise dramatically from the Atlantic Ocean, offering spectacular views and refreshing walks.

Across the border in County Galway, the area around the town of Gort has a number of historic (not to mention powerful) literary associations.

Lady Gregory, cofounder of the Abbey Theatre, lived in **Coole Park**, now a national forest with a heritage center. The novel "autograph tree" here is inscribed with the initials of some of her famous visitors—Augustus John, John Masefield, Sean O'Casey, and one of the very few who is instantly recognized by his initials: George Bernard Shaw.

Six km (four miles) northeast of Gort, William Butler Yeats bought himself a 16th-century tower, **Thoor Ballylee**, and decided to live there. The ideal place for inspiration, you can wander around this piece of romantic architecture with its spiral stairwell, alcoves, and just outside the window, its very own burbling stream.

Galway

The main city of the western province of Connacht, **Galway** (population 51,000) is a port, resort, administrative and cultural center. In medieval times it prospered as a city-state, but withered in the 17th century after two disasters: prolonged sieges by the forces of Thomas Cromwell and, four decades later, by William of Orange. However, remnants of the old glory still shine in a few corners of the renewed city.

The **Collegiate Church of St. Nicholas** (belonging to the Church of Ireland) was begun by the Anglo-Normans in the year 1320. Following the local tradition, Columbus came to pray here before his voyage to America, and the locals like to think he was checking out the sixth-century transatlantic explorer, St. Brendan. There is a pyramid-shaped steeple on top of the triple-naved church, full of stone carvings.

During Galway's heyday 14 families, mostly of Welsh and Norman descent, formed a sort of medieval Mafia that controlled the economic and political life of the town. Their common enemy, the O'Flaherty family, inspired the inscription (1549) over the old town gate: "From the fury of the O'Flaherties, good Lord deliver us." Of the countless "tribes" in Galway, the Lynch family left the most memories and monuments.

Lynch's Castle, a town house dating from 1600, is decorated with some excellent stonework, gargoyles, and carved window frames. This rare building has now been lovingly restored and houses a bank.

Another reminder of the Lynches is the "Lynch Memorial Window" with a plaque recounting the macabre story of James Lynch FitzStephen—Mayor of Galway in 1493—who condemned and executed his own son, Walter, for murder. Judge Lynch had to be the hangman because nobody else would agree to carry out the sentence. It was this incident which, it is said, inspired the expression "to be lynched," but it must be a wildly

County Galway offers plenty of quaint beauty, including this idyllic spot near Gort.

devious derivation, as the crowd in fact wanted to save Walter, not hang him.

Galway's Catholic cathedral—whose full name is **Cathedral of Our Lady Assumed into Heaven and St. Nicholas**—has a giant dome looming over the city. The classical architecture is misleading; the church was dedicated in 1965.

Alongside the cathedral is Galway's **Salmon Weir**, in which the salmon fight their way from the sea up to the lakeland. From June to July you can see them queueing up for a chance to leap up the falls and follow their instincts to sweet water.

In Galway you can also visit the restored house of **Bowling Green**, the one-up, one-down dwelling where James Joyce's wife, Nora Barnacle, was brought up.

Galway's seaside suburb, **Salthill**, is a hugely popular resort with many rocky seawalls and beaches of fine sand, which are ideal for a walk. It's a great place to watch the sun set on Galway Bay; sprawling hills enclose almost all of this immense bay, but the Atlantic Ocean can be seen and sensed to the west.

Connemara and the Aran Islands

Lough Corrib, which extends 43 km (27 miles) north from Galway, is big enough to be whipped by waves when the sudden wind hurtles down the hillside. It's generally shallow and well supplied with islands and fish—salmon, trout, pike, and perch. Lough Corrib divides County Galway into two contrasting regions: to the east a fertile limestone plain, and to the west Connemara, a range of dramatic mountains and a series of sparkling lakes, all enclosed by the coastline of fjords and pristine beaches.

Much of Connemara is an Irish-speaking enclave. This is the home of the Connemara pony—robust, intelligent, and self-reliant. Spanish horses of the 16th century are rumored to have crossbred with Irish ponies; one version says that the stallions swam ashore from ships of the Spanish Armada wrecked on nearby rocks.

The sky seems to change by the minute in the far west—dazzling sun, fleeting clouds, and rain alternating so quickly that photographers have to be constantly at the ready. But the resulting photos are definitely worth the effort in a land of thatched, white, stone cottages, and 180-degree rainbows.

The so-called "capital" is the well-placed market town of **Clifden**, a base for exploring the nearby lakes and rivers, as well as fine beaches, bogs, and mountains. The town's Irish name is *An Clochan*, meaning "Stepping Stones." There are in fact so many areas of water around Clifden that you can't tell the genuine sea inlets from the coves of the lakes, except for the seaweed, a plant which, incidentally, also features in Irish cooking.

Killary Harbor, near Leenane, offers superb anchorage which is protected by very high mountain walls on both sides. The floats and rafts, which look as if they belong to an oil project, are actually busy with farming mussels.

Funnily enough, the Irish don't think much of seafood, so it is generally exported to France where there are more true seafood enthusiasts.

The huge **Twelve Bens** of Connemara (*ben* is Gaelic for "peak") constitute a range of moody mountains which are inhabited mostly by sheep; the foothills are interspersed with bogs and pretty lakes.

Now for some real escapism. Out in the Atlantic, 48 km (30 miles) off Galway, the **Aran Islands** are a last bastion of peace and quiet and unbroken tradition. Their tall, handsome population, with strong, open faces, survive on a land so harsh that every blade of grass seems a miracle. They raise sturdy cattle, catch fish, and spin, weave, and knit. Aran sweaters are sold all over the country, but only here can you be sure it's the genuine, handmade article.

Inishmore, "the Big Island" as the Aran folk call it, is about 14 km (9 miles) from tip to tip and only 3 km (2 miles) across. From the air—and you can fly there from Galway— you see a tight gridwork of stone fences enclosing pockets of meagre pasture. In some fields you can even see the rock just beneath the grass.

Inishmore's one and only real village, **Kilronan**, has a port where ferryboats from the mainland dock. The fishermen work aboard modern trawlers, but the traditional *currachs,* tar-coated boats with canvas hulls, are still used. Kilronan's heritage center gives a good insight into island life. This is an island to explore on foot or rented bicycle. If you're in a hurry, you can hire pony traps for guided tours, or the island even has a single motorized taxi which doubles as a school bus.

The most remarkable monument here is **Dún Aengus**, a giant prehistoric fortress on the sheer edge of a cliff some 91 m (300 ft) high. It's about a 15-minute walk from the road, across unobtrusively marked fields. Three layers of stone walls, the outermost 6 m (20 ft) high, surround the courtyard 46 m (150 ft) across. With the ramparts and obstacles set up

Connemara is home to the Connemara pony, as well as Kylemore Abbey, nestled in the green hills of County Galway.

beyond the wall, the total area covers 4 hectares (11 acres). Even in modern times it would take a rash general to stage an attack on Dún Aengus.

Elsewhere on the islands, among the colorful, delicate wildflowers, grazing cows and sheep, and an abundance of bounding rabbits, there are numerous **archaeological sites**, which are of less importance, but which nevertheless have their own diversion to offer. Here you'll find stone forts and groups of primitive stone dwellings, as well as hermits' cells, round towers, and several ruined churches.

In striking contrast to these and other similarly traditional structures, a big glass-walled factory situated in the west of Inishmore exports its products to the many corners of the world where they are in demand. The time-honored dexterity of the Aran women has been fully diverted from the local, hardy wool to modern technology; nowadays they spend all their time making electronic components. They all speak Irish, but most people on the islands can speak English as well. Whether they greet you with *"Failte"* or "Welcome," they will all have a friendly greeting for strangers.

County Mayo

Rising high above Clew Bay, **Croagh Patrick** is Ireland's Holy Mountain. Compared to Ireland's other mountains, this holy peak looks more like a black slag heap. Even so, each year thousands of pilgrims ascend the imposing summit.

St. Patrick is said to have spent Lent here in 441. There are views of the bay and the hills of counties Mayo, Clare, and Galway. The town of **Westport**, at the head of Clew Bay, is an example of 18th-century urban planning. The Mall boulevard follows the Carrowbeg River, and the town's main plaza is an elegant octagon.

Outside the town, the home of the Marquess of Sligo can be visited from April to October. **Westport House** is pala-

From Bog to Stove

In this energy-hungry world it sounds too good to be true: you go to a field, dig up the moist topsoil, dry it, and then burn it for cooking, heating the house, even generating electricity. Of course, in real life it's not so easy, but peat, the typically Irish fuel, does produce about half the heat of coal.

Locally known as turf, peat is found in the bogs which cover one-sixth of the country. It is created by centuries of interaction between the bog's water and vegetable matter. After the bog is drained, the turf is cut into uniform chunks, stacked for drying, and eventually collected for use. A typical family burns 12 to 15 tons a year.

Now city slickers can even buy peat briquettes to burn in their fireplaces to create the sweet nostalgic smell of Ireland.

tial, with paintings, silver, and glassware. There's a souvenir shop, go-cart rides for children, and even a dungeon.

Inland, the village of **Knock** (from the Irish *Cnoc Mhuire* —"Mary's Hill") is a respected place of pilgrimage. In 1879 the townspeople saw an apparition of the Virgin Mary, St. Joseph, and St. John on a south gable of the old parish church. The centenary year reached its climax when the pilgrim Pope John Paul II came from Rome to address an open-air mass at Knock with at least 400,000 of the faithful.

Getting here is easy now that the international airport is in operation. Knock also caters to the pilgrims, with souvenir shops and a museum of folklore and handicrafts.

A new **basilica**—Ireland's biggest church—was built in advance of the anniversary; it can hold 20,000 worshippers. The small parish church is still there, but the **south gable** had to be restored after much of the mortar was taken away as relics. The site of the famous apparition has been enclosed in glass, and statues recreate the position of the figures in the vision.

In the town of **Foxford**, an interpretative center tells the story of the old woollen mills and the famine in the area, while near Ballycastle, on the north Mayo cliffs, the new pyramid-shaped heritage center of **Céide Fields** reveals the ancient history of the many prehistoric settlements in the area. The site is estimated to be the single largest Stone Age monument in existence in the the world today. It dates as far back as 3000 B.C.

The country's biggest island, **Achill**, is buffeted by wind and tide, with meagre farms between ominous mountains and rocky shores. It feels adrift, though you can drive there from the mainland across a short and unimpressive bridge.

Driving on Achill's wide open and deserted roads can revive the joy of motoring. But even if the traffic were heavy, the truly magnificent scenery—from 244-m (800-ft) cliffs to superb beaches—would still be worth the trouble.

Near Keel, **Trawmore Strand** is an outstanding model of a long, white-sand beach. Keel's large nine-hole golf course spreads to the dunes and so suffers no shortage of bunkers.

Prehistoric graves can be found on the harsh slopes of Achill's overpoweringly high mountain, the 672-m (2,204-ft) **Slievemore**. Driving offers the most dizzying cliff views and perspectives from the ocean churning round the off-islands and shoals. Inland, note the three-chimneyed cottages set between moors and bogs.

THE NORTHWEST

Sligo (population 20,000) lies between two mountains, Ben Bulben and Knocknarea.

Early fame came to Sligo in 807 when the Vikings invaded. In 1252 Maurice Fitzgerald, the Earl of Kildare, founded **Sligo Abbey**, a Dominican friary. It was accidentally burned down in 1414, but rebuilt soon afterwards. Then it suffered an attack by Puritan troops in 1641, and the friars were killed. Its ruins combine desolation with grace. Three sides have been preserved, and there are excellent carvings.

The resort **Strandhill**, west of Sligo, has a beach with long-rolling waves for surfers. **Knocknarea**, the flat-topped mountain over this stretch of shore, must have had a strange attraction for the early settlers.

The area has an abundance of megalithic monuments and on the 329-m (1,078-ft) summit of Knocknarea there is a *cairn* (tomb of stones). Legend says it is the burial place of the first-century Queen Maeve of Connaught. Facing Strandhill, on the opposite side of the harbor, are the resorts of Rosses Point and **Coney Island**, after which, it is said, New York's amusement park was named.

W.B. Yeats is buried near the front door of the town's small church, with its turreted belfry in the shadow of the awesome **Ben Bulben**, 527 m (1,730 ft) high. On its flat top you'll find arctic and alpine plants.

About 27 km (17 miles) to the north of Sligo, situated on the approach to the village of Mullaghmore, look out for the stunning **Classiebawn Castle**, which claims the skyline all to itself. This was the summer dwelling of Earl Mountbatten of Burma, who was assassinated by the IRA in 1979 when his fishing boat was blown up just off the shore nearby.

County Donegal

The most northerly county on the island, Donegal is known for its scenery—mountains, glens, and lakes. This is where the Donegal homespun **tweed** comes from.

Donegal's medieval **castle** occupies the site of a previous Viking fort. (*Dun na nGall* in Irish means the "Fortress of the Foreigners," a reference to the Vikings.) On the edge of town, the ruins of Donegal Abbey overlook the estuary.

Westward along the coast, **Killybegs** is a big-time fishing port; the trawlers here have wheelhouses with devices for tracking down the fish.

The road to the village of **Glencolumbkille** heads deep into spectacular country. Over the crest of a hill, you see the simple village below, enfolded in green hillsides that funnel down to the sea. In Irish the name *Glencolumbkille* means the "Glen of St. Colmcille" (or St. Columba). Today it is said that the sixth-century saint, who changed the course of history by introducing the Christian faith to Scotland, began his career by converting locals. The numerous old **standing stones** were formerly pagan monuments which St. Columba simply adapted to the new religion. On the saint's feast day, 9 June, pilgrims follow the pathway of these old stones. Over 40 prehistoric *dolmens, souterrains,* and *cairns* have been catalogued in this area, some as old as 5,000 years.

The gravestone of W.B. Yeats stands steps away from the small church of Sligo.

Set between Derry and Letterkenny, you can visit the **stone fort** built in prehistoric times, which is well-preserved and similar in style to Staigue Fort in County Kerry (see page 65). Fort Dunree on the Inishowen peninsula overlooking Lough Swilly is a fascinating military history museum in an old fort.

Glenveagh National Park forms 10,000 hectares (24,710 acres) of the most beautiful part of Co Donegal, including Glenveagh Castle and Glebe House, which was built in 1828 in graceful Regency style and sumptuously furnished. It was once the home of Derek Hill, the artist, who gave it to the Irish nation.

NORTHERN IRELAND

The Union Jack flies over six of the nine counties forming the ancient province of Ulster, a fact which has caused fiery feelings in the Irish people for decades. Although these feelings are still given expression by certain activist groups, the peace process has radically affected daily life in Northern Ireland. The difference is particularly noticeable in central Belfast where most of the security measures have been lifted. Beyond the city, the scenery of exuberant rolling hills, with its lovely lakes, and a grandiose coast, remains the same, unaware and unscathed.

Here are the main attractions of Northern Ireland:

The **Antrim Coast Road** is a marvel of the 19th-century skills in technical engineering. It hugs an impressively scenic coastline, beneath white cliffs, beside beaches, through quaint villages, and under craggy rockfaces.

The seascapes to be seen here may be splendid, but the nine idyllic **Glens of Antrim** along the way, with their many green forests, dancing waterfalls, and streams, are the stuff of legends.

One of the candidates for the title "eighth wonder of the world," the **Giant's Causeway** is Ireland's most amazing natural phenomenon. Molten lava was frozen into some 38,000 basalt columns, most of which are hexagonal, and these form the tightly packed "stepping stones" out into the sea. This vast, spectacular oddity, some 60 million years old, excites the imagination of even the most cynical observer. Some of the individual formations have names like the Honeycomb, the Chimney Pots, and the Wishing Chair.

Nearby at **Port na Spaniagh**, a Spanish Armada ship was wrecked in 1588. Nearly four centuries later Belgian divers recovered an incredible king's ransom in gold, silver, and jewels, the best of which are now on view at the Ulster Museum in Belfast.

Ulster's indefatigable statisticians can't say how many lakes there are in **County Fermanagh**, but they have counted an astonishing 154 islands in the 80-km (50-mile) stretch of Upper and Lower Lough Erne. "Fisherman's paradise" is the appropriate subtitle for Fermanagh, and no wonder—in 1979, a now famous angler named Dennis Willis managed to pull in an incredible 93 kg (207 pounds) of fish in just five hours. Millions more roach, pike, perch, and bream are still available on this shore, and there is no closed season on coarse fishing.

In Northern Ireland's most imposing range, compact but aloof, the 15 granite peaks of the **Mourne Mountains** tower more than 610 m (2,000 ft) over the land below. At the summit

Giant's Causeway—a.k.a. Honeycomb, Chimney Pots, and Wishing Chair.

of Slieve Donard you will find two *cairns* (ancient mounds of stones). From here, on a flawless day, you can see Scotland, England, the Isle of Man, and Snowdonia in Wales.

Much livelier than its name might indicate, the **Ulster Folk and Transport Museum** enjoys a grand total of 70 hectares (172 acres) of the greenest woodland park. Old farmhouses, mills, and even a church were all moved with painstaking labor, stone by stone, from their original sites all over Ulster to be preserved in one spot—the agricultural, industrial, and social history of the province. In the transport section you can admire ancient carriages and bicycles, as well as cars and aircraft. The new Railway Gallery houses an array of steam locomotives and old carriages.

Ulster Museum, a modern site in Belfast itself, also looks out onto a beautiful park, the Botanic Gardens. The art department features Irish and British painting up to the present day, while the archaeological exhibits begin with prehistoric Irish artifacts and continue through to working relics of the Industrial Revolution which transformed Belfast from a village to the metropolis it is nowadays.

Navan Fort, near Armagh, is a most important Celtic site in Europe and was the seat of the ancient kings of Ulster. It offers a visual and interactive display which children will enjoy.

WHAT TO DO

SPORTS

Whether on land or sea (or river or lake), the Irish enjoy so many sporting possibilities that we can only touch on a handful of the big favorites. If you are interested in more esoteric sports, such as hang-gliding, orienteering, or even polo, the tourist board can put you in touch with the appropriate sports associations.

Sports Ashore

Golf: In a country so green, you might scarcely notice the vast number of golf courses, but, amazingly, there are more than 600, including several of championship status. Some clubs are private, but do not despair. While you might find that nonmembers are excluded over the weekend, you'll have no problems on weekdays. In between rounds you can always keep in shape with pitch and putt, a traditional Irish game somewhere between minigolf and the real thing, played with a putter and one other club.

Greyhound racing: This is a very popular pursuit on the island. Teams of hare-brained dogs keep eager gamblers busy six nights a week in Dublin—which has two greyhound stadiums—and elsewhere in Ireland.

Horse racing: Almost everyone in Ireland seems to be totally engrossed, one way or another, in the Sport of Kings. Dublin boasts one track, and several famous courses within easy reach on a day-trip. The flat season is from March to November, and steeplechasing goes on all year.

Horse riding: Stables can be found all over Ireland with fine Irish horses, beautiful ponies, and trekking routes through delightful verdant countryside.

Tennis: Many hotels advertise their own courts, some of them with instructors, but elsewhere there are public courts, including those in many Dublin parks.

National games: Hurling is a very fast variant of hockey, in which a small, leather-covered ball is struck with a "hurley," similar to a hockey stick.

Gaelic football, that other very traditional Irish game, includes elements of both soccer and rugby.

Imported games: Soccer, rugby, and even cricket are also widely played.

Sports on the Water

Sailing: Any seasoned old salt with a seaworthy yacht will no doubt welcome the challenges of the west coast, but first-time sailors will be better off handling conditions off the south and east coasts and in the bays all around the island. Ask the tourist board for details about boat rental and sailing fees.

Sea fishing: From a long sandy beach, a pier, a clifftop, or a boat, you too can hook big beautiful trophies of the deep, such as shark, sea bass, tope, skate, halibut, conger, and many more.

Swimming: The tourist board's information sheet on seaside resorts lists a dozen—not bad for such a modestly sized island. The beaches come in all shapes and sizes, but have one thing in common: no crowds.

Surfing: The heavy Atlantic swells are more impressive on the west and north coasts, and so offer better surfing.

Boating: Cruising on a river is very popular. You can also try more energetic sports such as canoeing on lakes or rivers.

Game fishing: Fertile salmon fisheries are mostly restricted, but arrangements can be made—though preferably well in advance. Trout are abundant in rivers and lakes; as with salmon, you will need a licence.

SHOPPING

Friendly sales staff help make shopping in Ireland a real pleasure. Shopkeepers are so sincere here that they'll even advertise a competitor. The appealing products here are made by Irish craftsmen in traditional or new styles.

Aran sweaters: These fishermen's sweaters can be easily recognized. Demand so far exceeds the supply that they are now made in mainland factories as well as in the cottages on the Aran islands. Be sure to check if it is genuinely handknitted.

Connemara marble: A rich green, this stone is made into all sorts of souvenirs.

Crafts: An array of enamel dishes, plaques, and pendants by local craftsmen.

Crosses: Reproductions of old Christian crosses, and St. Brigid crosses made out of straw.

Dolls: Dressed in traditional regional costumes.

Glassware: Waterford crystal, world renowned, is once again a busy concern. Crystal is also made in Kilkenny, Tipperary, Cavan, Dublin, Galway, and Tyrone.

Jewelry: Celtic designs and illustrations from the Book of Kells inspire today's goldsmiths and silversmiths.

Kinsale smocks: These hardy cotton wind-cheaters are made for local sailors—not to be

Horse riding is one of many great outdoor activities to be enjoyed in Ireland.

A glass etcher pays special attention to the intricate demands of his work.

confused with Kinsale cloaks, traditional dress now revived as chic evening-wear.

Lace: Although a waning trade in Limerick and County Monaghan, there is now a strong revival of lace-making in Carrickmacross, Clones, Kenmare, and Youghal.

Linen: Weaving continues in Northern Ireland, is sold everywhere in the country.

Paintings: Many Irish-based artists produce fine studies of Ireland, including landscapes, seascapes, flora, and fauna, in oils, watercolors and pen and wash. These works are widely available and well priced.

Peat: Even the turf of Ireland is now compressed and sculpted into reproductions of ancient religious and mythical folklore symbols.

Pottery: Both traditional and modern designs in tableware and ovenware.

Rushwork: In a land rich with thatched cottages, the makers of woven baskets and similar wickerwork are still working in a thriving business.

Smoked salmon: A souvenir you can eat that is specially packed for traveling, and on sale at the airport.

Souvenirs: Leprechauns in all sizes, pretty "worry stones" of marble, as well as elegant Irish coffee glasses, and *shillelaghs* (short wooden clubs) are all widely available. Books, published in Ireland, about every aspect of Irish life and its history, make easy-to-carry souvenirs.

Tweed: Handwoven fabrics in a variety of bright and subtle colors and weights, ideal for overcoats, jackets, drapes, or light shawls.

NIGHTLIFE

Many hotels and pubs present cabaret nights featuring the most diverse cross section of traditional Irish entertainment possible: folk singers, harpists, dancers and storytellers. In local pubs the program may consist of a lone folk singer with guitar. At the other end of the scale the luxury hotels put on elaborate productions.

The shows have a typically Irish mixture of hand-clapping high spirits and "Come Back to Erin" nostalgia. Jigs and reels are tirelessly danced, and lively tap dancers revive some of the country's oldest and best routines. Harps and banjos are plucked and bagpipes and accordions squeezed. Fast fiddlers are as ubiquitous here as gypsy violinists in Budapest, though they tend to be a lot more cheerful.

You will find less polished versions of traditional Irish music at *fleadhanna*, festivals of music and song around the country, climaxing in the all Ireland *Fleadh* in the summer (August). Tourist offices will have detailed schedules of such events.

Dublin has a lively **nightclub** scene, with music for all tastes. Lower Leeson Street, the leading nightspot, has become somewhat passé with **Temple Bar** in the city center becoming more appealing to younger crowds seeking entertainment. The more up-to-date nightclubs usually offer witty and fast-talking DJs or other artists, food, drink, and very often a celebrity or two from the worlds of film and music.

Restored medieval castles are used for another kind of night out—grandiose candlelit **banquets** with traditional

stories, poems, and songs. These re-creations of lusty celebrations from the past are professionally arranged. If you
have no car you can join package tours that include door-to-
door transportation.

Ireland's grand **theatrical** tradition—which gave the world
Goldsmith, Shaw, Sheridan, Becket, O'Casey, and Behan—
continues in some major towns such as Dublin, Belfast, and
Cork. The Abbey Theater, Dublin is still "packing them in"
after more than 75 years. Newspapers usually print full list-
ings of theatrical events as well as concerts and films.

CHILDREN IN IRELAND

Fun activities for children of all ages can be found throughout the country at:

Bray promenade, 19 km (12 miles) south of Dublin. A
big seaside resort with dodgems, and a seafront aquarium.

Captain Venture, Level 3,
The Square, Tallaght, Dublin
22, Tel. (01) 459 6039.
Amusements for children up
to 13.

Clara-Lara, Vale of Clara,
County Wicklow, Tel. (0404)
46161. Fun park, trout farm,
and amusements for children
of all ages.

Dublin Zoo, Tel. (01) 677
1425. A wide variety of animals. Café and restaurant.

*Holding hands in Galway
—for children, Ireland can
be a walk in the park.*

Farm visits. In numerous regions farms are open to visitors and offer a warm welcome to children. Tourist information offices have full details.

Fota Wildlife Park and Arboretum, near the town of Cobh, County Cork, Tel. (021) 481 2678. Large wildlife park, open mid-March–October.

Fun Factory, Monkstown, County Dublin, Tel. (01) 284 3344. An activity center for children up to the age of 12.

Irish National Heritage Park, near Wexford, Tel. (053) 20733. Full-sized replicas of buildings from prehistoric to Norman times. Open mid-March–October.

Kilmainham Gaol, Dublin, Tel. (01) 453 5984. An historic jail converted into a history and heritage center. Open all year, every day.

National Gallery of Ireland, Merrion Square West, Dublin 2, Tel. (01) 661 5133. Frequent children's activities. Web site <www.nationalgallery.ie>.

National Wax Museum, Franby Row, off Parnell Square, Dublin 1, Tel. (01) 872 6340. Wax figures, Chamber of Horrors.

Newbridge Demesne, County Dublin, Tel. (01) 843 6534. An 18th-century house with farm and animals.

Straffan Steam Museum, in County Kildare, Tel. (01) 628 8412, has model and full-sized steam engines.

The **butterfly farm** in County Kildare, Tel. (01) 627 1109 has a large number of butterflies as well as scary, hairy tarantulas and myriad other poisonous spiders. Open in May, June, July only.

Tralee, in Co. Kerry. Steam train runs from the town to Blennerville, a restored early 19th-century windmill only 3 km (2 miles) away.

Westport House, Westport, County Mayo, Tel. (098) 25430. There are play facilities for children, plus a zoo and a steam railway.

CALENDAR OF EVENTS

As dates frequently change, we advise you to contact the local tourist office for up-to-date information on particular festivals.

March: *St. Patrick's Week*—celebrations in Dublin and other towns throughout the country.

April: *The Cork International Choral Festival*. The famous Irish Grand National horse race; *Dublin International Film Festival*.

May: *Cork International Choral and Folk Dance Festival; Dublin Spring Show and Industries Fair; Dundalk Maytime Festival*—classical music in great Irish houses (late May); *Killarney Pan-Celtic Week*—competitions and cultural events which enjoy the participation of other Celtic countries; *Listowel Writers Week*—takes place in County Kerry.

June: *Festival of Music in Great Irish Houses*—classical concerts.

July: *International Folk Dance Festival*—held in Cobh. *Dún Laoghaire Festival*—held in County Dublin; *Galway Arts Festival and horse races; Irish Open Golf Championships*.

August: *Dublin Horse Show*—the top event of the year; *Connemara Pony Show*—held in Clifden, County Galway; *Kilkenny Arts Week; Moynalty Steam Threshing Fair*—held in County Meath; *Oul Lammas Fair*, Ballycastle, County Antrim; *Puck Fair*—three days and nights of non-stop Irish entertainment, Killorglin, County Kerry; *Stradbally Steam Rally*—staged in County Laois.

September: *National Football and Hurling Finals*—Dublin; *Festival of Light Opera*—staged in Waterford; *Rose of Tralee Festival*—an international event (see page 66).

October: *Kinsale Gourmet Festival*—staged in County Cork; *Dublin Theater Festival*—new plays by Irish authors and companies from abroad; *Cork International Film Festival; Wexford Opera Festival*, shows of rare operas; *Ballinasloe Fair* (Europe's oldest horse fair), County Galway; *Cork Jazz Festival*.

November: *The International Horse Show* (Dublin)—a major event of the international equestrian calendar.

EATING OUT

Hearty meals are served in a baffling array of places—from hotels and bars to coffee shops and snack bars, from pubs to restaurants. "Pub grub" tends to be hot or cold meat pies, sandwiches, and simple salads, while restaurants run from the most modest to the truly elegant, with prices to match. Dublin is increasingly sophisticated in its array and quantity of restaurants, and the city is matching other European capitals as a breeding ground of talented and innovative chefs.

Keep in mind the 'businessman's lunch," a package deal at many provincial and city restaurants, usually involving a set three courses for a fraction of the cost of an evening meal. This is worth considering if you are traveling with a limited budget.

In addition to VAT (value added tax), a lot of restaurants add a service charge to the bill; extra tips are rare.

When to Eat

Breakfast is served from about 7am–10am, though in some hotels, matching the general leisurely air, it does not begin until 8am. Lunchtime is from 12:30pm–2:30pm, give or take half an hour at either end.

The hour—and name—of the evening meal depends on who and where you are. In

I'll have an olive—choices aplenty at the English Market in Cork City.

rural areas and perhaps the less sophisticated town areas, people dine as early as 6pm. and refer to the evening meal as "tea." In the major towns and cities, however, you can have your "supper" any time from 6 or 7pm–11pm.

What to Eat

Breakfast

A real Irish breakfast starts the day superlatively. You'll feel ready for any kind of exertion after a menu of juice, porridge, or cold cereal with milk or cream, fried eggs with bacon and sausages, toast or tasty homemade soda bread, butter, marmalade, tea, or coffee. Irish soda bread, white or brown, is made from flour and buttermilk, bicarbonate of soda, and salt; it's as delicious as cake.

What a way to start the day—a real Irish breakfast is just what you need to fuel a few hours of exploring.

Other meals

Irish **soups** are usually thick and hearty: vegetables, barley, and meat stock with a dab of cream, for instance. Look for potato soup made of potatoes, onions, carrots, and parsley.

Fish caught fresh from the Atlantic, the Irish Sea, or the island's streams is incredibly good. Keep an eye out for some of these great Irish delights: fresh salmon (poached or grilled), smoked salmon, sole, and trout from the sea and rivers. Dublin Bay prawns are a big natural resource worthy of their fame, as are Galway oysters (often accompanied by a bottle of stout). With luck you could be offered mussels or lobster, but the great bulk of the catch is usually exported to the Continent.

Meat of the highest quality is at the center of Irish cuisine. The beef is excellent, but there is very little veal. You'll have a choice of sumptuous steaks (either T-bone, filet mignon, or sirloin), or roast beef. Lamb appears as tender chops or as a roast, or the main ingredient in Irish stew, a filling casserole of meat, potatoes, carrots and onions, laced with parsley and thyme. Irish pork products—bacon, sausages, chops, and Limerick ham—are also rightly famous. Dublin Coddle is a delicious stew of sausages, bacon, onions, potatoes, and parsley, a favorite for Saturday night supper in the capital.

Vegetables as basic as the potato play a big part in Irish cooking. Potatoes have been a mainstay of the Irish diet since the 17th century. Mushrooms, which thrive in the cool, humid atmosphere here, are the single biggest horticultural export. More and more restaurants are now serving vegetarian dishes.

Desserts are often similar to sticky English "puddings"—trifles, *gateaux,* and generally very sweet offerings, sometimes with a scrumptious topping of thick cream.

What to Drink

A pitcher of tap **water** is often found on the table, and for many diners it's the only drink during the meal. Ireland has many brands of bottled spring water, widely sold and served in pubs and restaurants, and water is gaining popularity as a substitute for alcoholic drinks, especially at lunchtime. Wine is popular in Ireland as links with Europe have strengthened. By a quirk in the law, restaurants licensed to serve sherry and wine cannot serve spirits or beer, but the Irish don't see beer as a dinner accompaniment anyway.

Irish **pubs** are usually as relaxed and friendly as their regular clients. Although the eccentric licensing hours used to mean that public houses in the Republic's urban areas had to close between 2:30 and 3:30pm, this "holy hour" no longer exists, and most pubs are open all day, but they are still closed on Sunday afternoons. The pubs in Northern Ireland are permitted to open on Sundays, but not all choose to do so.

The Irish drink nearly 500 million pints of **beer** a year, mostly stout—a rich, creamy, dark brown version. Cork's two brands of stout, Beamish and Murphy's, have become increasingly popular.

In many a pub the simple order "a pint, please" means 568 ml of **Guinness**, lovingly drawn from the keg, scraped, and topped. The "head" is so thick the barman can sculpt it with his spatula like a baker icing a cake. A "glass" of stout means half a pint. Irish lagers and ales are less filling, and are also worth trying. An interesting Irish drink, **Black Velvet**, combines stout and champagne, and is said to be good for hangovers.

The word **whiskey** comes from the Gaelic *uisce beatha*, "water of life." (Purists are at pains to spell Irish whiskey with an "e" unlike the Scottish version). Whiskey is matured in wooden casks for at least seven years and is drunk neat, or

The way things used to be—old barrels of Irish whiskey stand on display at the Old Jameson Distillery.

with a little water—never with ice. Enthusiasts can visit the world's oldest whiskey distillery, Bushmills, in Northern Ireland; it has held a license since 1609. Also, the Old Jameson Distillery is an award-winning destination in Smithfield, the heart of old Dublin.

Whiskey figures in some unusual and delicious drinks: **Irish Coffee**, in a stemmed glass, is hot coffee laced with whiskey and sugar, with a tablespoonful of thick cream floating on top. Two Irish liqueurs merit a try: **Irish Mist** —honey and herbs in a whiskey base—tingles on the palate, and **Irish Cream Liqueur**, in different brands: there's Bailey's and Carolan's, Sheridan's and St. Brendan's. It contains whiskey, chocolate, and cream, like a leprechaun's milkshake.

HANDY TRAVEL TIPS

An A–Z Summary of Practical Information

A

ACCOMMODATION (See also CAMPING, YOUTH HOSTELS, and the selection of RECOMMENDED HOTELS starting on page 126)

While exploring Ireland you can stay in a varied combination of different accommodation: a super-luxury hotel one night, a family-run guest house the next, a farmhouse and a thatched cottage after that. Efficient tourist offices will handle both spur-of-the-moment or long-range reservations for you. The tourist boards are responsible for inspecting and classifying all hostelries, issuing brochures free or at minimal cost, and for listing the various approved establishments available with information about their rates and facilities. Tariffs are government-controlled, and the maximum rate shown in the brochure is the highest which proprietors may charge.

Hotel bills usually include a service charge, and you will find that VAT (value added tax) on the total cost of accommodations, meals, and service is included in the tariffs.

Hotels and motels. These are graded by the tourist authorities into five different star ratings.

***** Most luxurious with high standard of cuisine and services.

**** Extremely comfortable with experienced service.

*** Well-furnished, offering a good service; a private bath available but not necessarily in the majority of rooms.

** Well-kept, limited but good cuisine and service.

* Clean and comfortable, hot and cold running water.

Guesthouses. Usually family-run with friendly personal service, these can include full board for resident guests, and are also listed and graded by stars (one to four). Make sure that you enquire prior to booking about the full services offered.

Irish Homes. The Irish Tourist Board issues three informative books: *Be Our Guest, Bed & Breakfast,* and *Irish Farmhouse Holidays*, which cover a full range of hotels, guesthouses, and youth hostels, as well as town and country homes and farmhouses. The

Ireland

Northern Ireland Tourist Board publishes two similar brochures. As for finding Bed and Breakfast accommodations, you don't need any brochures to find them—you'll see signs all over the place.

Thatched Cottages. This plan operates mainly in western Ireland near famous beauty spots in five counties. The details are available from tourist offices or Rent-an-Irish Cottage Ltd., O'Connell Street, Limerick; Tel. (061) 411109.

AIRPORTS
International flights arrive at six airports, in the east, south, west, and north: Dublin, Cork, Kerry, Shannon, Knock, and Belfast.

Dublin Airport, 11 km (7 miles) north of the capital, is the busiest. Coaches link the airport with Busaras, the city bus terminal, every 20 minutes. The trip takes about half an hour. Taxi time between the airport and central Dublin is also about half an hour.

Dublin Airport has all the amenities that international travelers look for, including a porter service and push-it-yourself trolleys. Other facilities include a bank, car-rental offices, a church, hairdresser, nursery, post office, and tourist information offices, as well as a hotel-reservation desk, bars, restaurants, and shops (including a duty-free shop).

Shannon Airport, one of the first Atlantic gateways, is situated about 24 km (15 miles) to the west of Limerick. All usual facilities are available, as well as a vast and varied duty-free shopping area.

Belfast Airport (Aldergrove) is 24 km (15 miles) west of the city center. There is a bus service into town every 80 minutes.

B

BICYCLE RENTAL (See also MONEY MATTERS)
A network of dealers all over the island encourages bike rental as a way of seeing "the real Ireland." Children's and adults' models, racing bikes, and even tandems are all available. Tourist information

offices have a leaflet listing dealers in more than 100 towns from Antrim to Cork. Motorbikes and mopeds cannot be rented in Ireland.

BUDGETING FOR YOUR TRIP

To give you an idea of what to expect, here's a list of average prices in Irish pounds.

Accommodations: luxury hotel (double room, bath, and breakfast) €100–200. Medium hotel (double room, bath, and breakfast) €50–100. Guesthouses (double room with bath) €30-60. In town and country homes and farmhouses, bed and breakfast costs €20-30.

Airport transfer: bus to Dublin ¤5, taxi to central Dublin €20 + tip.

Babysitter: €8 per hour.

Bicycle rental: €45–60 per week, plus deposit.

Buses: local fares €1.65 (to the most distant suburb). An 8-day bus/rail rambler ticket for unlimited cross-country travel costs €145, an 8-day ticket (bus only) restricted to the Republic of Ireland is €135, an 8-day bus/rail ticket for the Republic and Northern Ireland is €168, a weekly bus/rail ticket for the greater Dublin area costs €24.

Camping: €10–15 per night.

Car rental (international company): Rentals can begin at $40 per day/ $200 per week (US$) and go to $60 per day/$320 per week with unlimited mileage.Add 12.5 percent tax in the Republic, 17.5% tax in Northern Ireland.

Cigarettes: €4 per packet of 20.

Entertainment: Movie tickets cost €6–9. Admission to discotheques and nightclubs are €5–15 or more. Theater tickets are €15–25.

Ferry: Galway-Aran Islands €19 roundtrip.

Meals and drinks: set-price lunch €10, dinner €15–45, add a carafe of wine at €15, soft drink €2, pint of beer €3, whiskey €2.

Museums, stately homes: €5 admission.

Taxis: minimum charge, Dublin €5, O'Connell Street to Heuston Station €8, Merrion Square to St. Patrick's Cathedral €8. You may find a supplement is payable for extra passengers, baggage, etc.

Tours: Dublin city sightseeing, half-day €12. Cork bus tour to the Ring of Kerry €24.

Trains: Dublin–Cork €44.40. A 5-day rail explorer ticket for unlimited travel is €98.

C

CAMPING (See also MONEY MATTERS)

Officially-approved campsites range from spartan to luxurious, but if a "no vacancy" sign is posted, take heart: many a farmer will let campers spend the night on his property, but you should always ask first. At some campsites, and at rental agencies, touring caravans (trailers) can be rented. If you're pulling your own, note that the connections for Calor gas tanks are not suitable for the cylinders sold in Ireland. Lists of camping and caravanning parks and their various facilities are available from tourist information offices or the Irish Caravan and Camping Council, P.O. Box 4443, Dublin 2. Contact the Northern Ireland Tourist Board at North Street, Belfast BT1 1ND59; Tel. (028) 9024 6609; web site <www.ni-tourism.com>.

Horse-drawn caravans may be rented by the week, if you want to get a taste of the gipsy life. They are most commonly found in the west and south west of Ireland. Bookings should be made in advance through the Central Reservation Service, Irish Tourist Board, Baggot Street Bridge, Dublin 2; Tel. (1850) 230 330; web site <www.ireland.travel.ie>.

CAR RENTAL (See also DRIVING IN IRELAND and MONEY MATTERS)

Dozens of car rental companies operate at airports and in the towns, dealing in everything from minicars to so-called executive cars and vans. The internationally known firms usually have slightly higher rates than their local competitors, but you may find that booking from abroad might get you better value for money. Some companies permit cars to be picked up in one place and handed in elsewhere.

Most companies have a two-tiered tariff, raising prices by up to 10 to 20 percent for the summer season. In any season, cars may be rented on a "time-plus-mileage" basis or with unlimited mileage, but if you're unsure whether you'll be chalking up enough traveling to justify the "unlimited" rate, the firm may agree to let you choose the more favorable tariff retroactively. Investigate before you travel.

A valid national license, normally at least two years old, will be required. Many firms permit 21-year-old drivers to rent cars, but the minimum age can be as high as 25. The maximum age, depending on the company, ranges from 65 to 70. Credit cards are normally accepted in lieu of a deposit.

Rental rates include third-party liability insurance. Additional coverage can be arranged on the spot, and comprehensive coverage is recommended.

Don't forget: drive on the left and wear your seat belt at all times.

CLIMATE and CLOTHING

The Gulf Stream is credited with keeping the Irish weather mild year-round, but the unexpected can happen with readings as cold as -2°F (-19°C) and as hot as 92°F (33°C) recorded over the past century. May is usually the sunniest month of the year, and December the dullest.

Average monthly temperatures in Dublin:

	J	F	M	A	M	J	J	A	S	O	N	D
°F	41	41	43	47	51	56	59	58	56	50	45	43
°C	5	5	6	8	11	13	15	14	13	10	7	6

Temperatures do not vary much from north to south, but the weather in the west and southwest can be a good deal more wet than elsewhere because the winds come in over the land direct from the sea, bringing moisture with them. It may be wise, therefore, to pack some light protective clothing for the summer, and certainly warmer items in the winter.

Ireland

In the winter the Wicklow Mountains near Dublin, Donegal in the northwest and County Kerry in the southwest have heavy snowfalls, making the territory dangerous even for the most seasoned walkers and climbers. Therefore wear hardy, warm and protective clothing and follow the proper code by informing the hotel owners of your route and time of return—and take some provisions with you.

COMMUNICATIONS (See also TIME DIFFERENCES)

Post Offices. The Post operates all mail services offered in the Republic. Most mailboxes are pillar-shaped (a few antiques still have Queen Victoria's monogram on them), and are painted green. Most post offices are open from 9am–5:30pm, but the main one—the historic General Post Office in O'Connell Street, Dublin—is open 8am–8pm Mon–Sat, and 10:30am–6:30pm on Sundays. Postcard shops and newsstands sometimes sell stamps too. In some areas a post office may be identified by a sign in Irish only—*Oifig an Phoist*.

If you don't know where you'll be staying, you can have mail sent to you "poste restante" (general delivery) to any town. Letters sent "poste restante" to the GPO in Dublin may be collected up to 8pm.

In Northern Ireland the mailboxes are red. Note that Republic of Ireland stamps may not be used on mail posted in Northern Ireland and British stamps are invalid in the Republic.

Telegrams. In Ireland the traditional telegram has been replaced by the telemessage. Dial 196 and it will be delivered the next day. The telemessage is accepted at post offices, with similar delivery speed.

Telephones. Public telephones are found in post offices, hotels, stores, and on the street. In the Republic sentry-box booths—cream with green trim—and modern aluminium and glass booths are increasingly used. They are marked in Gaelic, *Telefon*.

Instructions for operating coin telephones are usually given. Payphones in Ireland use 10¢, 20¢, and 50¢ and €1 coins for direct dialling of local, national, and international calls. Many payphones use calling cards, which can be bought from local post offices and shops. Operator assistance is available by dialing 10.

In Northern Ireland, public telephones are found in metal and glass booths or yellow cubicles. They operate with 10p, 20p, 50p, and £1 coins as well as phonecards. Do not deposit money until the connection has been made; a series of rapid beeps will indicate when the machine is ready to accept your coins.

COMPLAINTS

Your first move, of course, should be to complain to the manager of the offending establishment. If this fails to give satisfaction, turn to your nearest tourist office.

Complaints in writing may be directed to the Customer Relations Section, Irish Tourist Board, Baggot Street Bridge, Dublin 2; Tel. (1850) 230 330, or the Northern Ireland Tourist Board, 59 North Street, Belfast BT1 1NB; Tel. (028) 9024 6609.

You could also contact the Consumers Association of Ireland Ltd., 45 Upper Mount Street, Dublin 2; Tel. (01) 661 2466; web site <www.consumerassociation.ie>.

CRIME (See also EMERGENCIES and POLICE)

The Crime Prevention Office of the Garda Siochana (police) warns visitors to carry a minimum of cash and jewelry. Pickpockets do operate in stores and public places. Tourists who leave property unattended risk losses. Park in well-lit, busy areas and keep valuables out of sight. Thefts from hotel rooms are rare.

CUSTOMS and ENTRY FORMALITIES

Citizens of many countries do not require visas. British travelers directly from Britain require no passport or identity card, but others should present valid documents. Visitors from countries infected with yellow fever will need proof of vaccinations. It is forbidden to import pornographic material or books listed by the Republic of Ireland government's censor. You may bring unlimited European currency into the country, but you may only take out up to 100 euros, unless travelling to another "euro-zone" country. Foreign currency brought in can be taken out, plus the equivalent of 500 euros (travelers' checks excluded). This does not apply to people traveling between Ireland and Great Britain, the Channel Islands, or the Isle of Man.

Residents of European countries with non-tax free goods bought in the EU can bring into the Republic 800 cigarettes or 200 cigars or 1kg of tobacco, plus 1.5*l* spirits and 5*l* wine. European residents with tax-free goods can bring in 200 cigarettes or 50 cigars or 250*g* tobacco plus 10*l* spirits and 90*l* wine. Residents of non-European countries can bring in 200 cigarettes or 50 cigars or 250*g* tobacco, plus 1*l* spirits and 2*l* wine.

The customs restrictions between the Republic and Northern Ireland are normally limited to animals and agricultural products. Since the peace process began, most of the previously unauthorized or blocked border crossings have been reinstated, and there are no longer any security checks.

D

DRIVING IN IRELAND (See also CAR RENTAL and EMERGENCIES) Traffic moves on the left. Beware: some road-signs are in Gaelic only.

Importing your car. Be sure to have the registration papers and insurance coverage. The usual formula is the Green Card, which is an extension to the normal insurance, making it valid in other countries. Your car should also have a nationality plate on the back. Virtually any valid driving licence from any country is recognized in Ireland.

Driving conditions. If you're not accustomed to driving on the left, be careful for the first few days, especially when turning corners and at traffic circles (roundabouts). Driving on country lanes can be a pleasurable experience, but be alert for the unexpected: you could find cattle camped in the road, tractors inching along, and ambling pedestrians blocking your way. On zebra crossings (marked by amber beacons), pedestrians have the right of way. Beware of bicycles weaving in and out of town traffic; cyclists make their own rules here.

Speed limits. Unless otherwise marked, the speed limit in the Irish Republic is 96km/h (60mph) on the open road, and it is set at 48 or 64km/h (30 or 40mph) in towns and built-up areas. On motorways the limit is 112km/h (70mph). In Northern Ireland the limit in towns is 48km/h (30mph), 96km/h (60mph) in the country, and 112km/h (70mph) on motorways.

Parking. This is becoming more difficult, especially in Dublin and other big cities. Parking meters in Dublin generally have instructions printed on them. Some towns have zones requiring "discs" or other variations on this time-limit system. Check the signs for the regulations that apply.

If you leave your car on a yellow line during business hours you may be fined for parking in a no-parking zone. If you leave your car on a double line, meaning "no waiting" (regardless of time or day), it may be towed away, and you will have to pay a fine plus towing charges.

Fuel. In some areas finding a filling station open on a Sunday may be a problem, so it's best to top up on Saturday for weekend excursions. Gas (petrol) is sold by the liter.

Fluid measures

Distance

Seat belts. Drivers and front-seat passengers must wear seat belts in the Republic; failure to use them may be punished by a fine. If a vehicle is built with rear seat belts, it is compulsory to use them.

Drinking and driving. Police on both sides of the border are strict about this. Any driver suspected of being affected by drink will be subjected to a roadside breathaliser test. Those who fail—and it only takes a pint or two of beer—risk heavy fines, or jail, or both. The crackdown affects visitors as well as residents.

Road signs. Many international picture-signs are used on highways. The road direction signs in the Republic are mostly in English and Gaelic, but in Irish-speaking enclaves the English may be omitted. Traditional road signs give distances in miles and, increasingly, in kilometers.

Some signs may not be comprehensible to visitors:

Ireland	*U.S.A.*
Clearway	No parking along highway
Cul de sac	Dead end
Dual carriageway	Divided highway
Layby	Rest area
Level crossing	Rail crossing
Loose chippings	Loose gravel
No overtaking	No passing
Road up	Under construction
Roadworks	Men working
Soft edges (or **margin**)	Soft shoulder

E

ELECTRIC CURRENT

In Ireland the standard current everywhere is 220-volts, 50-AC, but you will find that hotels usually have special sockets for shavers, running at both 220 and 110 volts.

Note that it is possible for certain appliances to need a converter, and also that adapter plugs may be required to fit into Ireland's two types of wall outlets. These can be either three-pin flat or two-pin round.

EMBASSIES and CONSULATES

The Dublin telephone directory lists foreign embassies and consular services under the heading "Diplomatic and Consular Missions."

Consular agencies in provincial towns are all listed in Part 2 of the directory under the same heading.

The details of the principal embassies and consulates in **Dublin** are as follows:

Australia: Fitzwilton House, Wilton Terrace, Dublin 2; Tel. (01) 676 1517; web site <www.australianembassy.ie>.

Canada: 65/68 St Stephen's Green, Dublin 2; Tel. (01) 478 1988; e-mail <cdnembsy@iol.ie>.

Great Britain: Merrion Road, Dublin 4; Tel. (01) 205 3700; web site <www.britishembassy.ie>.

US: 42 Elgin Road, Dublin 4; Tel. (01) 668 7122; web site <www.usembassy.ie>.

In Northern Ireland:

US: Queen's House, 14 Queen Street, Belfast BRT1 6EQ; Tel. (028) 9032 8239.

EMERGENCIES

(See also EMBASSIES and CONSULATES, MEDICAL CARE, and POLICE)
To contact the police, fire department, or an ambulance in an emergency, dial **999** from any telephone in Ireland (no coin required), and tell the emergency operator which service you need. Have details of your location ready before you make your call.

G

GAY and LESBIAN TRAVELERS

Nowadays the general attitude of younger people in Ireland tends to be tolerant towards gays and lesbians, but some travelers may find there is a slightly more socially conservative attitude in the southern parts of Ireland and some of the more provincial or remote areas of the country.

Various organizations provide advisory services for gay people. They include the Gay Federation/Gay Community News, Dublin; Tel. (01) 671 0939; web site <www.gcn.ie>, and the Gay Christians Switchboard at Tel. (01) 872 1055. Also, NIGRA (Northern Ireland

Ireland

Gay Rights Association) holds weekly meetings. For information write to NIGRA, c/o PO Box 44, Belfast BT1 ISH; or call the organization on Tel. (028) 9066 4111 or (028) 9086 5257.

There are also a number of counseling organizations:

Gay Switchboard, Dublin; Tel. (01) 872-1055. Open 8–10pm Sunday to Friday, and 3:30–6.30pm Saturday.

Lesbian Line, Dublin; Tel. (01) 872-9911. Open 7–9pm Thursday.

GETTING THERE
It is advisable to consult a travel agent for the latest information on tariffs and other arrangements as well as writing to the local tourist offices for information in advance.

From Great Britain

By Air
Visitors and tourists can fly in from airports across the U.K. to Dublin, Shannon, Cork, Kerry, Waterford, and Knock in the Republic and to Belfast International, Belfast City, and Derry airports in Northern Ireland. New routes are opening all the time, so it may be worth checking with the airline of your choice for information on the most convenient connections to Ireland.

Charter Flights and Package Tours. A wide array of packages is currently available for visitors, making good use of the varied vacation accommodations Ireland has to offer—whether it be cottages and farmhouses, driving your own horse-drawn caravan, cruising down the river, or other, more traditional forms of self-catering accommodations, there will be something in Ireland for everyone.

Some airlines offer fly-drive tours, as well as special fares which may include your flight and all the transport to and from your final destination in Ireland. Check with the airline of your choice.

By Sea
Passenger and car ferries sail frequently from Holyhead to Dublin and Dún Laoghaire. There is also a regular service from Fishguard

and Pembroke to Rosslare Harbor, and from Swansea to Cork. Ferries shuttle several times a day from Cairnryan and Stranraer to Larne (near Belfast). A daily catamaran service runs between Stranraer and Belfast.

Those touring Ireland without a car might want to buy a rambler ticket (5 days rail travel, 8 days bus/rail travel, or 15 days bus travel) or an overlander ticket (which will allow you 15 days of bus and rail travel, including Northern Ireland on just the one ticket), which can be bought either at home or in Ireland from *Bus Éireann* or *Iarnród Éireann-Irish Rail*. *InterRail Passes* are valid for 15 or 30 days in Europe for those under 26 and for senior citizens over 65.

FROM NORTH AMERICA

By Air

Travelers from almost every major American city and several major Canadian cities can make connections to Dublin or Shannon through New York or Boston. Regular services are also available to Knock.

Charter Flights and Package Tours. Charter flights to Shannon, with connections to Dublin, feature even further air-fare reductions. The tourist boards have full details of charter flights.

GUIDES and TOURS

Guided tours are conducted at some major attractions as part of the admission fee, and a variety of excursions are led by guides, covering major monuments and beauty spots by bus. Tourist offices have schedules; the Dublin office has a list of qualified guides.

L

LANGUAGE

English is spoken with lilting Irish accents everywhere in Ireland. In the Gaeltacht areas of the west and south, the principal language is Irish, though most people speak fluent English too. Bilingualism is officially encouraged in the Republic. Summer courses in the Irish language are given in the Gaeltacht.

Ireland

Write to Comhdhail Naisiunta na Gaeilge, 86 Sraid Gardner Iocht, Baile Atha Cliath 1, Republic of Ireland.

Here is a short Irish glossary to help you read the signs:

Irish/Gaelic	*English*
ar(d)	high place
áth	ford of river
baile, bally	hamlet, group of houses, town
beann, ben	mountain peak
cairn	mound of stones on top of a prehistoric tomb
carrick, carrig	rock
cather	fort
clachan, clochan	small group of dwellings; stepping stones across a river; beehive-shaped hut
clon, cluain	meadow
corrach	marsh or low plain
corrie	circular hollow with steep sides
currach	small boat
derry, dare	oak tree or wood
donagh	church
drum, drom	ridge, hillock
dun, doon	fort
ennis, inch, innis(h)	island
keel, kill, caol	narrow
kil, kill, cill	church; monk's cell
lough	lake, sea inlet
mol, mull	height
ros	promontory or wood

sceillig, skellig	crag, rock	
sliabh, slieve	mountain	
tulach, tully	hillock	

And here are a few phrases to help you in general, with a rough guide to pronunciation:

Dia dhuit	hello	*diah guich*
slán	goodbye	*slawn*

(many people in Ireland also say "good luck" meaning "goodbye")

oiche mhaith	good night	*e-ha wah*
go raibh maith agat	thank you	*goh rev moh a-gut*
le do thoil	please	*leh doh hol*
tá fáilte romhat	you're welcome	*taw faltcha rowet*
sláinte!	cheers!	*sloyn-tcha*
gam pardún	excuse me	*gum par-doon*
Cá bhuil an ... ?	Where is the ... ?	*koh will on*

LAUNDRY and DRY CLEANING

Hotels in Ireland provide laundry and cleaning services. They often charge extra for "express" service. There are launderettes, dry cleaning establishments and self-service launderettes in most towns, and you can usually arrange a "service wash" for a small extra charge.

LOST PROPERTY

The first place to go in search of lost property is the local police station. However, public transport organizations sometimes have their own lost property departments. For items you may have left by accident on trains or buses in Dublin, try the Dublin Bus Lost Property Office Tel. (01) 703 1321, or the Irish Rail Lost Property, Connolly Station, Amiens Street, Dublin 1; Tel. (01) 702 2363.

The main lost property office in Belfast is at Musgrave Street c/o the RUC (Royal Ulster Constabulary) Police Station; Tel. (028) 9065 0222.

MEDIA

Radio and Television. Radio Telefís Éireann (RTE) is state-run and the largest broadcaster in the Republic, though cable television has expanded the choice. Most programs are in English except for a few Irish or bilingual ones. Foreign films are sometimes shown in the original language with English subtitles. RTE operates three radio stations primarily in English, as well as Raidio na Gaeltachta with an all-Irish program. The BBC runs five radio stations in Northern Ireland, and there are also commercial channels aimed at audiences north and south of the border.

Transistors and car radios can pick up the principal radio stations of Europe; reception is best at night.

Newspapers. Two national morning papers are published in Dublin —the *Irish Independent* and the *Irish Times*. The *Cork Examiner* is also considered a national daily.

Northern Ireland has two morning dailies, the *News Letter* and the *Irish News*. Entertainment news is covered in the *Evening Herald* of Dublin, the *Evening Echo* of Cork, and the *Belfast Telegraph*. Sunday papers are also useful, and visitors will also find a what's on section in the fortnightly magazine *In Dublin*.

Britain's national daily and Sunday newspapers are sold almost everywhere in the country on the morning of publication. Leading newsagents in the major towns also sell European newspapers and magazines as well as American magazines.

MEDICAL CARE (See also Emergencies)

Residents of EU countries (formerly EC) are covered by reciprocal health care in Ireland, and visitors from mainland Europe should ensure that they bring a completed E111 form; no form is required for U.K. visitors. Other nationalities should have some form of hospital insurance—many package tours provide temporary policies.

Hotels usually know which local doctors are available, but in an emergency you can dial **999** to find a doctor on call. In Dublin at least one hospital is always open for emergency cases; again, the operator on 999 can tell you which hospital is on duty.

The Dental Hospital, 20 Lincoln Place, Dublin 2; Tel. (01) 662 0766, takes dental emergency cases from 9–11am and 2–4pm.

Pharmacies (chemists) operate during shopping hours. A few stay open until 10pm, and some from 11am–1pm or 10pm on Sundays.

MONEY MATTERS

Currency. The unit of currency used in the Irish Republic is the euro (€€; in Northern Ireland the British pound sterling (£) is used. Both are divided into 100 units. These units are called cents in the Republic, pence in the north. Banks everywhere on the island are accustomed to exchanging euros and pounds.

Euro banknotes are issued in €5, €10, €20, €50, €100 and also €500 denominations. Coins come in 1, 2, 5, 10, 20 and 50 cents and 1 and 2 euros.

Exchange facilities. All major banks and many building societies provide exchange facilities. Major post offices, including the GPO in Dublin, have a bureau de change. Some international travel agencies also change money and travelers' checks. Be sure to take along your passport as proof of identity when cashing travelers' checks (see also OPENING HOURS for further information).

The O'Connell Street Tourist Information Office in Dublin and the Cork Office in Grand Parade operate money exchange services. The Dublin office will change your money from 9am–5:15pm Monday to Friday, while the Cork office provides this facility from 9am–1:15pm and 2:30–5:15pm Monday to Friday.

Credit cards and travelers' checks are widely accepted in Irish shops, hotels, restaurants and car-rental firms. Cash points at banks throughout the island offer cash advances on major cards.

OPENING HOURS
The opening hours of shops and offices can vary from season to season and according to where they are located.

Shops in the cities are normally open from 9am–5:30pm Monday to Saturday; country towns have one early closing day. However, the big shopping centers often stay open until 9pm on Thursday and Friday. Smaller shops, particularly groceries and newsstands, often open on Sundays and many stay open until 11pm. Also, some Dublin suburbs have 24-hour shops, which are open all day and all night.

Offices and businesses mostly operate from 9am–5:30pm Monday to Friday. Tourist information offices are open from 10am–6pm with longer summer hours in the busiest places.

Banks. In general banks are open 10am–4pm Monday to Friday. Most towns have a late opening day once a week (Thursday in Dublin), when banks stay open until 5pm. You'll also find that many banks remain open over the lunch hour. In Northern Ireland banks are open from 10am–3:30pm. Outside Belfast, branches may close for lunch. The bank at Dublin Airport is open every day of the year except Christmas, from 6:45am–9pm in the winter and until 10pm in the summer.

Pubs. Licensing hours have been streamlined. In the Republic, the winter hours are 10:30am–11:30pm, with an extra half hour in summer. On Sundays all year, pubs are open from 12:30–2pm and from 4–11pm. In addition, there is half-an-hour drinking-up time in the evenings all year round. In Northern Ireland, pubs are open Monday to Saturday 11:30am–11pm, all year.

Sunday opening is a relatively new departure, and is followed by some pubs, which now open from 12:30–2:30pm, and from 7–10pm, all year. In addition, there is half-an-hour drinking-up time.

Museums, stately homes, etc. Museums and stately homes follow no general rule except that visiting hours will often be curtailed in winter.

There are no universal days when these institutions are closed, though Sunday, Monday, or Tuesday are the most probable. To avoid disappointment always check first with the nearest tourist information office.

P

PHOTOGRAPHY
All those green fields, blue skies and white clouds make beautiful pictures, but if you should run out of film, you'll easily find all the well-known brands on sale. Be sure to ask permission before you take photos in museums and historic churches; sometimes flashbulbs are forbidden. Military bases are off-limits to photographers. Please note that in Northern Ireland you should avoid pointing your camera, or anything else, at personnel or installations of the security forces.

POLICE (See also EMERGENCIES)
The civic guard (police force) of the Irish Republic is the Garda Siochana, known as the Garda (pronounced "gorda"). The Police Service of Northern Ireland performs similar duties in the North. In case of emergency, telephone 999, in both the Republic and Northern Ireland.

PUBLIC HOLIDAYS
Shops, banks, official departments, and restaurants are closed on public holidays. If a date falls on a Sunday, then the following Monday is taken in lieu.

In the Republic of Ireland and Northern Ireland:

1 January	*New Year's Day*
17 March	*St. Patrick's Day*
last w/e in May (movable date)	*Good Friday/Easter Monday*
25 December	*Christmas Day*
26 December	*Boxing Day*

In the Republic of Ireland only:

first Monday in June	*June Bank Holiday*
last Monday in August	*August Bank Holiday*

Ireland

last Monday in October	*October Bank Holiday*

In Northern Ireland only:

first Monday in May	*May Day*
last Monday in May	*Spring Bank Holiday*
12 July	*Orangemen's Day*
last Monday in August	*Summer Bank Holiday*

R

RELIGION

About 95 percent of the people in the Irish Republic are Catholic. Many go to Sunday Mass, which can be heard in Dublin almost any time, from 6am–9pm, in English, and sometimes in Irish.

Dublin's cathedrals are of the (Anglican) Church of Ireland, and schedules of the services at these and other Protestant churches can be found in hotels, and in Saturday papers. Dublin has Protestant, Greek Orthodox, Jewish, and Islamic places of worship.

In Northern Ireland, Catholics make up less than a third of the population, but they outnumber the largest single Protestant group, the Presbyterians, as well as the Church of Ireland.

The ecclesiastic capital of Ireland is Armagh, situated in the North with two cathedrals, one Catholic and the other Church of Ireland. Both are called St. Patrick's.

T

TIME DIFFERENCES

Ireland sets its clocks one hour ahead of GMT (Greenwich Mean Time) from mid-March to the end of October, but the rest of the year the clocks are set to GMT.

TIPPING

Most hotels and restaurants include a service charge, so tipping is unnecessary. However, good or extra service from bellboys, filling-station attendants, etc. deserves an appropriate extra gratuity.

TOILETS/RESTROOMS

Public conveniences abound in Irish towns, and are well signposted. The only hitch is that the gender signs on doors in the Republic may be printed in Gaelic, not English. *Mná* should not be misconstrued as a misprint for "men"; it's Gaelic for "ladies." *Fir* means "gentlemen."

TOURIST INFORMATION OFFICES

Tourist information offices all over Ireland provide full travel information and advice, booklets, maps, and a comprehensive hotel reservation service (for a small charge), which can extend to booking novel horse-drawn caravans and self-drive cabin cruisers. The offices are usually open from 10am–6pm, although many local ones operate only in the summer. For enquiries, write to one of the following:

Irish Tourist Board, Bord Fáilte, PO Box 273, Dublin 8; web site <www.ireland.travel.ie>.

Northern Ireland Tourist Board, St Anne's Court, 59 North Street, Belfast BT1 INB.

You may also address your enquiries to offices of the **British Tourist Authority** the world over.

TRANSPORTATION (See also MONEY MATTERS)

Buses. The state-run Bus Éireann operates an extensive network of local, provincial, and express bus routes, including full cross-border services in conjunction with Northern Ireland's Ulsterbus Ltd. The service to the various destinations of tourist interest is increased in the summer. You can buy a handy, pocket-sized timetable at bus stations and tourist information offices. *Bus Átha Cliath/Dublin Bus* runs Dublin Area Services. A separate book lists all bus and train routes in the Dublin district.

The bus services in Ireland cover almost every town and village. "Expressway" buses provide a non-stop inter-city service, while the so-called "Provincial" vehicles make frequent stops in rural areas.

Iarnród Éireann-Irish Rail and *Bus Éireann* sell rambler tickets allowing unlimited cross-country travel for 8 days (bus/rail) or 15 days (bus only). There is also an overlander ticket with 15 days of unlimited travel in the Republic, and with Ulsterbus and Northern Ireland Railways (see TRAINS below).

On some buses the destination is indicated in Irish only, so if you don't want to arrive in Gaillimh (Galway) instead of Gleann Garb (Glengarriff), you'd better learn the correct Gaelic name before you start out. You will find that the timetable book has a useful glossary.

The busiest bus routes in the cities use double-deckers, on which you take a seat and wait for the conductor to come and collect the proper fare. On single-deckers you must pay the driver as you enter. Queues (lines) are taken seriously, and you should note that in Ireland the official Queueing Regulations of 1961 rule that six or more persons waiting for a bus must form a double line in an orderly manner. The line should face the direction from which the bus will arrive, except where the bus stop sign indicates otherwise.

Trains. Passenger train lines in Ireland have been cut back to the main routes, but cross-country services to and from Dublin are both quick and comfortable. The main inter-city routes have air-conditioned, sound-proofed expresses.

There are two classes on through-trains: Standard (2nd class) and Super Standard (1st class). *Iarnród Éireann-Irish Rail* sells a 5-day rail ticket and an 8-day bus/rail ticket for unlimited travel in the Republic, and a 15-day bus/rail pass valid in the whole of Ireland. Train timetables are on sale at railway stations and tourist offices.

Note: Dublin has two main-line railway stations (Heuston Station and Connolly Station), as well as a commuter-line station, so be sure to check in advance for the correct terminal.

Some trip times on express trains:

Dublin–Belfast:	2 hr 10 min
Dublin–Cork:	2 hr 30 min
Dublin–Galway:	2 hr 50 min
Dublin–Waterford:	2 hr 35 min

Ireland has now joined the group of countries which are honoring the **Eurailpass**, a flat-rate unlimited mileage ticket, valid for any first-class rail travel in Western Europe outside the U.K. The **Eurail Youthpass** is similar to the Eurailpass, but offers second-class travel at a cheaper rate to anyone under 26. This ticket is available to visitors from outside Europe.

Taxis. Irish taxis may be found cruising the streets, but most park at designated stands waiting for clients. Taxis can also be contacted by telephone (see the classified telephone directory under *Taxicabs— Ranks and Shelters*).

Many towns have radio-dispatched taxis, but these usually charge extra for the mileage to pick up the client. Fares can vary from town to town. Dublin and Cork have metered taxis while smaller towns have standard fares or charges by agreement.

Very few Dublin taxi drivers have been known to add imaginary supplements to the fare. Note that you should pay only the charge on the meter plus, if applicable, supplements for extra passengers, additional luggage, waiting time, and trips on public holidays or after midnight.

Radio-cab dispatchers in Dublin can be reached on any of the following numbers; Tel. 676 1111, 668 3333, and 677 2222.

Boats and Ferries. With over 4,800 km (3,000 miles) of coastline and 14,480 km (9,000 miles) of rivers and streams, Ireland is a boater's paradise. You might rent a fishing boat to take advantage of the excellent fresh-water and sea fishing, or enjoy the country's scenic splendors in a rented cruiser (normally available with two to eight berths). No boating permit is needed for traveling on the Shannon, and all companies offer a free piloting lesson. Points of departure include Carrick-on-Shannon, Athlone, Banagher and Killaloe.

The rugged islands off the coast of Ireland are rich in folklore, antiquities, and eye-catching natural wonders (especially birdlife). The Irish Tourist Board issues an information sheet—*Island Boat Services*—listing numerous possibilities, including scheduled ferries. The Aran Islands are only a 30-mile steamer ride from Galway; and crossings can also be made from Rossaveal, May to September, and from Doolin in County Clare. If you wish to visit the islands in a rented boat, check that it's registered, which will mean it will have adequate insurance coverage.

Ireland

There are connections by air, as well, which are around 20 minutes. Garinish Island, which is noted for its exuberant vegetation, is only 10 minutes away from Glengarriff (County Cork). Bad weather may interrupt ferry services.

TRAVELERS with DISABILITIES
A lot of progress has been made in recent years to provide more facilities for travelers with disabilities. Ramps have been provided, giving access to many community buildings, and much of the public transport system has been geared up to welcoming people with disabilities.

The more modern city buses in Dublin have facilities for wheelchair users to board the bus, and trains have level entry access. Airlines are also friendly towards passengers with disabilities.

For advice and information, contact the **National Council for the Blind in Dublin**, tel (01) 830 7033, and the **National Chaplaincy for the Deaf**, also in Dublin, tel (01) 830 5744.

W

WEIGHTS and MEASURES
Length

Weight

Temperature

WOMEN TRAVELERS

Women traveling alone in Ireland need to be as cautious in some areas of Ireland's major cities as they are in comparable areas in the major cities in their own home countries.

To ensure your safety, take a friend with you if possible, or decide to travel through dark and lonely areas by taxi. Inform yourself in advance about the times of the last trains, buses, etc., and have enough funds with you to pay for the full cost of your return travel by taxi, if necessary. Also, take some relevant telephone numbers with you for taxis, the police, and some advisory organisations.

In Dublin, the area north of the River Liffey and west of the city center is best avoided at night if you are alone. Similarly, the centers of Cork and Limerick are best avoided at night by women traveling on their own.

For further information and helpful advice contact the **Women's Health Section of the Eastern Health Board** in Dublin, Tel. (01) 635 2345; web site <www.erha.ie>. Alternatively, you could write to the following prior to starting your journey:

Women's Aid, PO Box 791, Dublin 1; Tel. 1 800 341 900 (toll free), (01) 874 5302; web site <www.womensaid.ie>.

YWCA, 64 Lower Baggot Street, Dublin 2 (hostel), Tel. (01) 660 8452, and 49 St. John's Road, Sandymount, Dublin 4; Tel. (01) 269 4521.

YOUTH HOSTELS

The Irish Youth Hostels Association runs 50 hostels in the Republic of Ireland. Membership cards are required, and these are issued by national youth hostel associations overseas.

An official handbook is available from the **Youth Hostels Association (HO),** 61 Mountjoy Street, Dublin 7, Tel. (01) 830 4555; web site <www.irelandyha.org>.

There are a dozen youth hostels in Northern Ireland. Details can be requested from **Youth Hostel Information,** 22 Donegall Road, Belfast BT12 5JN; Tel. (028) 9032 4733; web site <www.hini.org.uk>.

Recommended Hotels

Ireland has a huge selection of accommodations. Every location offers budget accommodations, and bed and breakfast can cost as little as €15 per night. For €40 a night, hotels can be luxurious. Those registered with Bord Fáilte, the Irish Tourist Board, have guaranteed standards. Some hotels, like Ashford Castle, Dromoland Castle, and Waterford Castle offer luxury at €300–€600 per night.

Self-catering accommodations are developed and are often easily rented, although it may be more difficult in peak months.

The international star system awards top hotels 5 stars and 1 star to modest hotels. Guesthouses get 1 to 4 stars.

Local tourist information offices have details of offers in their area. Hotel prices are subject to 12½ percent VAT.

Price categories for a double room at high season:

€€€	over 200 euros per night
€€	100 to 200 euros per night
€	under 100 euros per night

DUBLIN

Blooms Hotel €€€ *6 Anglesea Street, Dublin 2; Tel. 671 5622; fax 671 5997.* Located in the Temple Bar area. Restaurant, bar, and basement nightclub; parking lot. 86 rooms. Major credit cards.

Buswells Hotel €€€ *Molesworth Street, Dublin 2; Tel. 676 4013; fax 676 2090.* Centrally located (opposite the National Museums complex), set in a former Georgian townhouse. Rooms are all en suite. Restaurant and bars. Conference facilities. All major credit cards.

Castle Hotel € *3/4 Gardiner Row, Dublin 1; Tel. 874 6949; fax 872 7674.* Three fine restored Georgian buildings, close to Parnell Square. En suite rooms with phone, TV; parking lot. Major credit cards.

Central Hotel €€–€€€ *1–5 Exchequer Street, Dublin 2; Tel. 679 7302; fax 679 7303.* A comfortable, refurbished Victorian building in a central location, with dining room and bars. All major credit cards.

Clarence Hotel €€€ *6-8 Wellington Quay, Dublin 2; Tel. 670 9000; fax 670 7800.* Centrally located adjacent to Temple Bar, overlooking the River Liffey. Uniquely designed, en suite rooms. Restaurant, nightclub and elevator. 50 rooms. All major credit cards.

Conrad International Dublin €€€ *Earlsfort Terrace, Dublin 2; Tel. 676 5555; fax 676 5424.* Situated just off St. Stephen's Green, this glass construction opposite the National Concert Hall has 191 rooms.Two restaurants, a pub, and full business and conference facilities. All major credit cards.

Davenport Hotel €€€ *Merrion Square, Dublin 2; Tel. 661 6800; fax 661 5663.* An elegant lemon-colored building dating from the 1860s and set in a prime location. En suite rooms. Restaurant, bar, parking lot. All major credit cards.

Dublin International Youth Hostel € *61 Mountjoy Street, Dublin 7; Tel. 830 1776; fax 830 1600; <www.irelandyha.org>.* Budget priced accommodations in a converted convent. 350 beds. MasterCard, Visa.

Grey Door Guesthouse €€ *22-23 Upper Pembroke Street, Dublin 2; Tel. 676 3286; fax 676 3287,* Elegant, comfortable Georgian townhouse in harmonious surroundings near Fitzwilliam Square. Major credit cards.

Jury's Christchurch Inn €€ *Christchurch Place, Dublin 8; Tel. 454 0000; fax 454 0012.* Excellent location in the cathedral and castle area of the city (situated directly opposite Christ Church), this new hotel is geared to families. Comfortable accommodations at reasonable prices. Rooms are en suite. All major credit cards.

Longfield's Hotel €€–€€€ *9/10 Fitzwilliam Street, Dublin 2; Tel. 676 1367; fax 676 1542.* Excellent location in a splendid Georgian building near Merrion and Fitzwilliam squares. Lots of antique furniture. First-class restaurant. All major credit cards.

Mont Clare Hotel €€€ *Merrion Square, Dublin 2; Tel. 661 6799; fax 661 5663.* Conveniently located, an elegant hotel occupying a Georgian building. Restaurant, bar, parking lot. All major credit cards.

North Star Hotel €€ *Amiens Street, Dublin 1; Tel. 836 3136; fax 836 3561.,* A pleasant and well-run hotel in the city center, close to O'Connell Station. Parking lot. Major credit cards.

Royal Dublin Hotel €€ *40 Upper O'Connell Street, Dublin 1; Tel. 873 3666; fax 873 3120.* Convenient central location near Parnell Square. A modern hotel with an old world ambience. Restaurant and bars, parking lot. 117 en suite rooms. Major credit cards.

Russell Court Hotel €€ *Harcourt Street, Dublin 2; Tel. 478 4066; fax 478 1576.* Two Georgian houses make up this hotel. Harcourt Street runs south from St. Stephen's Green. Restaurant and bar. 52 en suite rooms. All major credit cards.

Shelbourne Hotel €€€ *27 St. Stephen's Green, Dublin 2; Tel. 676 6471; fax 661 6006.* Dublin's most famous hotel and certainly one of its most distinctive, with Art Deco Egyptian lampholders outside. Antique furniture, a very good restaurant and bar. Meeting rooms and parking lot. All major credit cards.

Staunton's on the Green Guesthouse €€–€€€ *83 St. Stephen's Green, South Dublin 2; Tel. 478 2300; fax 478 2263.* Exclusive Georgian house overlooking the green, very comfortably appointed. All rooms en suite with telephone. Major credit cards.

Temple Bar Hotel €€–€€€ *Fleet Street, Temple Bar, Dublin 2; Tel. 677 3333; fax 677 3088.* One of the city's newest hotels in a central location, near Grafton Street. En suite rooms, restaurant, and bar. All major credit cards.

Westbury Hotel €€€ *Grafton Street, Dublin 2; Tel. 679 1122; fax 679 7078.* A luxury city center hotel. Restaurants and bars, conference and business facilities, parking lot, and shops. 203 en suite rooms. All major credit cards.

Wynn's Hotel €€ *35/39 Lower Abbey Street, Dublin 1; Tel. 874 5131; fax 874 1556.* This city center hotel is just around the corner from the Abbey Theatre. Parking lot. 68 en suite rooms. Major credit cards.

CORK

Blue Haven Hotel €€€ *3/4 Pearse Street, Kinsale, County Cork; Tel. (021) 477 2209; fax (021) 477 4268.* Individually styled rooms, and a fine restaurant. Full Irish breakfast included. 17 rooms. Major credit cards.

Cork International Youth Hostel € *1 Redclyffe, Western Road, Cork; Tel. (021) 454 3289; fax (021) 434 3715; <www. Irelandyha.org>.* Inexpensive youth hostel. 102 rooms.

Fitzpatrick Cork €€€ *Tivoli, Cork; Tel. (021) 450 7533; fax (021) 450 7641; <www.morangroup.ie>.* Luxury hotel on eastern road to Cork City. Full Irish breakfast included. 109 rooms. Major credit cards.

Forte Travelodge €€ *Kinsale Road, Roundabout, South Ring Road, Blackash, Cork; Tel. (021) 431 0722 or 1 800 709709; fax (021) 431 0707.* Well-run, modestly priced modern family hotel.

Jurys Hotel Cork €€€ *Western Road, Cork; Tel. (021) 427 6622; fax (021) 427 4477; <www.jurysdoyle.com>.* Luxury-class accommodations and restaurants on west side of Cork. 185 rooms. Major credit cards.

Quality Hotel—Morrisons Island €€ *Morrison's Quay, Cork; Tel. (021) 427 5858; fax (021) 427 5833; <www. hotelchoice.com>.* Luxurious self-catering, en suite facilities, also has a restaurant. 56 rooms. Major credit cards.

Westlodge Hotel €€ *Bantry, Co. Cork; Tel. (027) 50360; fax (027) 50438; <www.westlodgehotel.ie>.* Modern hotel with all amenities. 100 rooms. Major credit cards.

GALWAY

Galway Great Southern Hotel €€€ *Eyre Square, Galway; Tel. (091) 564041; fax (091) 566704; <www.gsh.ie>.* 19th-century railway hotel. 106 rooms. Major credit cards.

KERRY

Benners Hotel €€ *County Kerry, Main Street, Dingle; Tel. (066) 915 1638; fax (066) 915 1412.* Comfortable hotel in the town center, with all amenities. Full Irish breakfast included. 52 rooms. Major credit cards.

Crutchs' Hillville House Hotel € *Connor Pass Road, near Castlegregory, County Kerry; Tel. (066) 713 8118; fax (066) 713 8159; <www.irishcountryhotels.com>.* Comfortable, rural atmosphere. Located near a lengthy, sandy beach. 19 rooms. Full Irish breakfast included. Major credit cards.

Doyles Seafood Bar and Town House € *John Street, Dingle, County Kerry; Tel. (066) 915 1174; fax (066) 915 1816; <www.doylesofdingle.com>.* This hotel is noted for its lively seafood restaurant. 8 rooms. Full Irish breakfast included. Major credit cards.

Sheen Falls Lodge €€€ *Kenmare, County Kerry; Tel. (064) 41600; fax (064) 41386; <www.sheenfallslodge.ie>.* Magnificent hotel in a setting to match; good facilities. Closed 2 January–2 February. 60 rooms. Major credit cards.

Towers Hotel €€ *Glenbeigh, County Kerry; Tel. (066) 976 8212; fax (066) 976 8260; <www.towershotel.com>.* Vintage inn, comfortably refurbished; with restaurant. 34 rooms. Major credit cards.

KILKENNY

Club House Hotel €€ *Patrick Street, Kilkenny; Tel. (056) 21994; fax (056) 21994; <www.clubhousehotel.com>.* Historic 18th-century hotel; mementoes include a set of witty 19th-century political cartoons. 37 rooms. Full Irish breakfast included. Major credit cards.

Foulksrath Castle Hostel € *Jenkinstown, County Kilkenny; Tel. (056) 67674; <www.irelandyha.org>.* Budget-priced youth hostel. 4 rooms (52 beds). Major credit cards; no American Express.

Hotel Kilkenny €€ *College Road, Kilkenny; Tel. (056) 62000; fax (056) 65984; <www.griffingroup.ie>.* Pleasant and modern hotel with all amenities, including a health and leisure center. Full Irish or Continental breakfast included. 103 rooms. Major credit cards.

Lacken House € *Dublin Road, Kilkenny; Tel. (056) 61085; fax (056) 62435; <www.lackenhouse.ie>.* Good bed and breakfast with widely acclaimed restaurant. Dinner included. 9 rooms. Major credit cards.

LIMERICK AND SHANNON

Ballyteigue House €€ *Bruree, Co. Limerick; Tel. (063) 90575; fax (063) 90575.* 18th-century Georgian farmhouse, all rooms en suite. Breakfast included. 5 rooms. Most major credit cards.

Carrygerry Country House €€ *near Shannon Airport, Newmarket-on-Fergus, County Clare; Tel. (061) 363739; fax (061) 363823.* Converted 18th-century house with rooms set around a courtyard, and a fine conservatory restaurant. Irish breakfast included. 12 rooms. Major credit cards.

Castletroy Park Hotel €€€ *Dublin Road, Limerick; Tel. (061) 335566; fax (061) 331117; <www.castletroy-park.ie>.* Ultra-modern hotel, all facilities. Breakfast included. 107 rooms. Major credit cards.

Dromoland Castle €€€ *Newmarket-on-Fergus, County Clare; Tel. (061) 368144; fax (061) 363355; <www.dromoland.ie>.* 19th-century baronial pile, now a luxury hotel in fine grounds. 99 rooms. Major credit cards.

International Hostel Limerick € *1 Pery Square, Limerick, County Limerick; Tel. (061) 314672; fax (061) 314672; <www.irelandyha.org>.* Youth hostel accommodations. 66 rooms. Major credit cards.

MAYO

Ashford Castle €€€ *Cong, County Mayo; Tel. (092) 46003; fax (092) 46260; <www.ashford.ie>.* Former 19th-century mansion of the Guinness family. The last word in luxury holiday accommodations. 83 rooms. Major credit cards.

Olde Railway Hotel €€ *The Mall, Westport, County Mayo; Tel. (098) 25166; fax (098) 25090; <www.anu.ie/railwayhotel>.* Very agreeable riverside hotel, full of artifacts and bonhomie; restaurant and pub serving food. 26 rooms. Breakfast included. Major credit cards.

Quiet Man Hostel € *Abbey Street, Cong, County Mayo; Tel. (092) 46089; fax (092) 46448; <www.quietman-cong.com>.* Budget accommodations. 15 rooms. Most major credit cards.

Ireland

WATERFORD

Granville Hotel €€ *Meagher Quay, Waterford; Tel. (051) 305555; fax (051) 305566; <www.granville-hotel.ie>.* Historic hotel by the River Suir. 98 rooms. Major credit cards.

Lismore Hostel € *Glengarra, Lismore, Co. Waterford; Tel. (058) 54390.* Youth hostel accommodations.

O'Grady's Restaurant & Guesthouse €€ *Cork Road, Waterford; Tel. (051) 378851; fax (051) 374062.* Bedrooms are all en suite. Michelin-recommended restaurant specializes in local seafood. Major credit cards.

Tower Hotel €€ *The Mall, Waterford; Tel. (051) 875801; fax (051) 870129; <www.towerhotelgroup.ie>.* Luxury hotel in the city center; amenities include an indoor swimming pool. Breakfast included. 140 rooms. Major credit cards.

Waterford Castle €€€ *The Island, Ballinakill, Waterford; Tel. (051) 878203; fax (051) 879316; <www.waterfordcastle.com>.* Historic castle, now a luxury hotel, with comprehensive facilities including a golf course. 19 rooms. Most major credit cards.

WEXFORD

Marlfield House Hotel €€€ *Gorey, County Wexford; Tel. (055) 21124; fax (055) 21572; <www.marfieldhouse.ie>.* Stylish country mansion recently converted into an exquisite hotel offering accommodations to a high standard, with gourmet restaurant. Full Irish breakfast included. 20 rooms. Major credit cards.

Rosslare Great Southern Hotel € *Rosslare Harbour, County Wexford; Tel. (053) 33233; fax (053) 33543; <www.gsh.ie>.* Modern hotel with all facilities. On clifftop overlooking seaport. 100 rooms. Major credit cards.

Whites Hotel €€ *George Street, Wexford; Tel. (053) 22311; fax (053) 45000.* Old-fashioned hotel brought up-to-date by renovation. Warm country-style ambience. Full facilities including health club. Breakfast included. 82 rooms. Major credit cards.

NORTHERN IRELAND

Belfast International Youth Hostel € *22 Donegall Road, Belfast BT12 5JN; Tel. (028) 9031 5435; fax (028) 9043 9699; <www. hini.org.uk>.* Modern, high-standard hostel accommodations in a central location. 38 rooms. Breakfast included. Major credit cards.

Bushmills Inn €€ *25 Main Street, Bushmills, County Antrim BT 57 8QA; Tel. (028) 2073 2339; fax (012) 6573 2048; <www.bushmills-inn.com>.* An old coaching inn converted into a comfortable hotel with its own historic character, and high quality accommodations. 32 rooms. Breakfast included. Major credit cards.

Chestnut Inn € *28 Lower Square, Castlewellan, County Down; Tel. (028) 4377 8247.* A well-established, 100-year-old family-run inn set in an attractive country town. 7 rooms. Major credit cards.

Culloden €€€ *142 Bangor Road, Holywood, County Down; Tel. (028) 9042 5223; fax (028) 9042 6777; <www.hastingshotels.com>.* Northern Ireland's most luxurious hotel, based on the shores of the Belfast Lough. 80 rooms. Major credit cards.

Belfast City Travelodge € *15 Brunswick Street, Belfast, BT2 7GE; Tel. (028) 9033 3555; fax (028) 9023 2999; <www. travelodge.co.uk>.* Hotel near the city's "Golden Mile" of nightclubs. Large, modern rooms. 90 rooms. Major credit cards.

Europa €€–€€€ *Great Victoria Street, Belfast BT2 7AP; Tel. (028) 9032 7000; fax (028) 9032 7800.* Next to the Grand Opera House, a 5-minute walk to the Golden Mile. Spacious elegance; stylish comfort. Restaurant, nightclub, parking lot. 185 rooms. Major credit cards.

Moohan's Fiddlestone € *1570 Main Street, Belleek, County Fermanagh; Tel. (028) 686 58008; e-mail <moohans@ infowing.ie>.* Traditional Irish guesthouse and pub in renowned pottery village.

Rathlin Guesthouse € *The Quay, Rathlin Island, Co. Antrim; Tel. (028) 207 63917.* The most isolated spot in Northern Ireland, this bed and breakfast offers the only accommodations on Rathlin Island. 5 units.

Recommended Restaurants

The choice of restaurants in Ireland has increased enormously over the last few years, with establishments offering Chinese, Indian, Japanese, Malaysian, and Thai cuisine opening up in many areas. A few restaurants serve authentic Irish food, like cabbage and bacon or Dublin coddle (bacon, kidney, sausage, and onion), but often hotels and guesthouses serve excellent, home-made food.

While Cork, including Kinsale, is acknowledged as one of the best areas for eating out, Belfast has developed hugely, and prices compete with those in the Republic. Some restaurants have a full licence to serve any drinks; otherwise, they serve wine only and not beer. Special tourist menus are a cheaper alternative for lunch and dinner.

The VAT rate on restaurant meals is 12½ percent. In addition, some restaurants may add a 12½ percent service charge. To give you an idea of prices, we have used the following symbols for a three-course meal for one excluding wine:

€€€	Over 20 euros
€€	10–20 euros
€	Under 10 euros

DUBLIN

Chapter One Restaurant €€–€€€ *18/19 Parnell Square, Dublin 1; Tel. 873 2266/873 2281.* This establishment, in the basement of the Dublin Writers Museum, is one of the city's best. Open for lunches (12–2:30pm, Mon–Fri) and dinners (6–11pm, Tues–Sat), pre-theater menus from 6pm. Reservations advised. Major credit cards.

Old Dublin Restaurant €€–€€€ *90/91 Francis Street, Dublin 8; Tel. 454 2028; fax 454 2346.* Specializing in Russian and Scandinavian recipes such as *novgorod* (beef chateaubriand with fried barley and caviar) and *pelmini* (small beef or veal dumplings in consommé), this is an unusual but long-established restaurant. Open 12:30–2:30pm, 6–11pm. Book in advance. Major credit cards.

Elephant and Castle €–€€ *18 Temple Bar, Dublin 2; Tel. 679 3121.* This is the most popular informal restaurant in the city. Quality burgers, salads, and meals with more than a hint of Mexican or Thai influence. Vegetarian options. Open 8am–12pm. Major credit cards.

Omar Khayyam €–€€ *51 Wellington Quay, Temple Bar, Dublin 2; Tel. 677 5758.* On the north side of Temple Bar by the Ha'penny Bridge, this small corner restaurant offers a vast range of Middle Eastern dishes like falafels, cous cous, and pita breads with a variety of fillings. Open noon–midnight. Major credit cards.

Well Fed Café € *Dublin Resource Center, 6 Crow Street, Dublin 2; Tel. 677 2234.* Award-winning vegetarian restaurant (a workers' co-operative) serving excellent food in generous portions at very cheap prices. Relaxed and very bohemian. Open 12:30–8:30pm.

The Bistro €€ *4 & 5 Castle Market, Dublin 2; Tel. 671 5430.* A young and informal Italian restaurant which serves a wide range of excellent dishes all day. Open daily noon–10:30pm.

Blazing Salads € *Powerscourt Townhouse Center (2nd floor), Clarendon Street, Dublin 2; Tel. 671 9552.* Delicious wholefood at tempting prices. A wide range of salads accompanies hot dishes like vegetable moussaka. Open 9:30am–6pm. No credit cards.

The Cedar Tree €€–€€€ *11a St. Andrew Street, Dublin 2; Tel. 677 2121.* Authentic Lebanese food at its best, reasonably priced. The decoration is exotic and the atmosphere unique. On weekends there is the added attraction of a belly dancer. Open 5:30–11pm.

Chompys € *Powerscourt Townhouse Center (2nd level), Clarendon Street, Dublin 2; Tel. 679 4552.* The menu's terrible puns describe a range of American-deli food. Toasted bagels, huge sandwiches, and an all- American breakfast served with coffee, and some wicked cakes. Open 8am–6pm Mon–Sat (until 7pm on Thurs).

Ireland

Cornucopia € *19 Wicklow Street, Dublin 2; Tel. 677 7583.* A small self-service vegetarian restaurant offering delicious meals like Turkish bean casserole, tasty salads, and wholemeal breads. Very good value and not to be missed. Open 9am–8pm Mon–Sat. Visa only.

Ernie's €€€ *Mulberry Gardens, Donnybrook, Dublin 4; Tel. 269 3300.* Interesting restaurant built around a mulberry tree, with the main dining room lined with contemporary Irish paintings. The cooking and presentation is classical, with charcoal grill, and seafood and game in season. Closed Sun–Mon. Major credit cards.

Pasta Fresca €€ *3/4 Chatham Street, Dublin 2; Tel. 679 2402.* A popular and relaxed restaurant, serving, as the name suggests, virtually every possible combination of pasta and sauce. Vegetarian options. Open daily 11am–11pm. Major credit cards.

Rajdoot Tandoori €€–€€€ *26–28 Clarendon Street , Dublin 2; Tel. 679 4280.* Award-winning Indian restaurant with a vast menu; much of it is suitable for vegetarians. You haven't eaten Indian food until you've eaten here. Open noon–2:30pm, 6:30–11:30pm. Major credit cards.

Jury's Coffee Dock €€ *Jury's Hotel and Towers, Pembroke Road, Ballsbridge, Dublin 4; Tel. 660 5000.* The value of the Coffee Dock, especially if you are staying in the Ballsbridge area, is that you know you can have a good, reasonably priced meal or snack at virtually any time of day or night. Open 22 hours a day. Major credit cards.

Cork

Ballymaloe House €€ *Shanagarry, Middleton, County Cork; Tel. (021) 465 2531; fax (021) 465 2021.* On a farm, the restaurant is run by the Allen family, noted worldwide for their gourmet writing. Open 1–1:30pm, 7pm–9:30pm. Major credit cards.

Café Paradiso €€–€€€ *16 Lancaster Quay, Western Road, County Cork; Tel. (021) 427 7939.* The best vegetarian restaurant in Ireland. Major credit cards.

Little Chef Restaurant/Forte Travelodge € *Kinsale Road Roundabout, South Ring Road, Blackash, Cork; Tel. (021) 431 0722.* Reasonably priced food in bright, clean surroundings. Open 7am–10pm. Major credit cards.

Mary Ann's Bar and Contented Sole Restaurant €€ *Castletownshend, Skibbereen, County Cork; Tel. (028) 36146; <www.golfer.ie>.* Seafood restaurant with cheaper menus served from the bar; the restaurant is set in a small, idyllic seaside village in West Cork. Open 11am–3pm, 6pm–midnight. Major credit cards, no American Express.

Presidents' Restaurant €€ *Longueville House, near Mallow, Co. Cork; Tel. (022) 47156; <www.longuevillehous. ie>.* An upmarket 18th-century mansion is the setting for this restaurant with walls lined with portraits of Ireland's presidents. Has its own vineyard, which produces a wine similar to a Riesling. Open 12pm–5pm, 6:30pm–9pm.

Shiro Japanese Dinner House €€ *Ahakista, Durrus, Co. Cork; Tel. (027) 67030.* Authentic and expensive Japanese cuisine; restaurant is small and very popular, so advance booking essential. Open 7pm–midnight. Major credit cards.

Galway

Brannagans Restaurant & Bar €€ *36 Upper Abbeygate Street, Galway; Tel. (091) 565974; fax (091) 567261; e-mail <cpbran@ indigo.ie>.* Boasting an exotic Victorian-style interior; Brannagans features fine multicultural cuisine. Major credit cards.

Currach Restaurant €€ *Corrib Great Southern Hotel, Dublin Road, Renmore Galway; Tel. (091) 755281; <www.gsh. ie>.* A restaurant with fine views overlooking Galway Bay. Open 7:30am–10:00am, 1pm–2:15pm, 6:45pm–9pm. Visa/MC.

Galleon Restaurant €–€€ *Beside the Church, Salthill, Galway; Tel. (091) 522963; fax (091) 581240.* Well-priced menu: fish, steaks, and Irish stew, all served in a seaside setting. Open daily noon–11pm. Major credit cards.

GBC Restaurant and Coffee Shop € *7 Williamsgate Street, Galway; Tel. (091) 563087; <www.gbcgalway.com>*. Inexpensive and centrally located, using as much fresh local produce as possible. Open 12pm–10pm. Major credit cards.

Oyster Room €€ *Galway Great Southern Hotel, Eyre Square, Galway; Tel. (091) 564041; <www.gsh.ie>*. Noted restaurant in center of the city, serving first-class cuisine. Open 7:30am–10am, 6:30pm–9:30pm (9pm on Sunday). Major credit cards.

Kerry

Beginish Restaurant €€ *Green Street, Dingle, County Kerry; Tel. (066) 915 1588*. Delicious French nouvelle cuisine in an elegant, understated setting. Closed Mondays. Major credit cards.

Doyles Seafood Bar & Town House €€ *John Street, Dingle, County Kerry; Tel. (066) 915 1144; <www.doylesdingle. com>*. One of the country's best-known restaurants. It's cramped, but it's also full of life and character—a fun place to eat. Open Mon–Sat 6–9:30pm. Major credit cards.

La Cascade, Sheen Falls Lodge Hotel €€€ *Kenmare, County Kerry; Tel. (064) 41600; <www.sheenfallslodge.ie>*. Imaginative and colorful menus using fresh local produce, served in a restaurant overlooking spectacular waterfalls. Open 7:30am–10am, 7:15pm–9:30pm. Major credit cards.

The Laurels €€ *Main Street, Killarney; Tel. (064) 31149*. A long-established and family-run restaurant serving very good food. The menu includes vegetarian and gluten-free dishes. Open May–Oct, 6–9:30pm Mon–Sat. Major credit cards.

Park Hotel Kenmare €€ *Kenmare, County Kerry; Tel. (064) 41200; <www.parkkenmare.com>.* First-class cuisine in an elegant 5-star hotel. Open 7–9:15pm. Major credit cards.

Pizza Time € *Innisfallen Shopping Center, Killarney; Tel. (064) 35380.* Friendly restaurant, with a warm atmosphere and fully licensed bar. Visa/MC.

Limerick and Shannon

Doolin Café € *Doolin, Co. Clare; Tel. (065) 74795.* A friendly, informal atmosphere is the hallmark of the Doolin Café in its seaside village location. It offers wholesome food, and good music as well as a range of books to browse through.

Earl of Thumond & the Fig Tree Restaurant Dromoland Castle €€ *Newmarket-on-Fergus, County Clare; Tel. (061) 368142; fax (061) 363355.* The dining room in Dromoland Castle is spectacular, with superb, elaborate table settings and grand chandeliers overhead; excellent backdrop for the gourmet cuisine. The Fig Tree restaurant offers a more relaxed setting. Major credit cards.

Lindbergh Restaurant €€ *Shannon Catering, Shannon Airport, County Clare; Tel. (061) 471444; fax (061) 472602.* Spacious restaurant with friendly staff, serving a good selection of traditional Irish dishes, including famous Limerick ham.

MacCloskey's €€ *Bunratty House Mews, Bunratty, Co. Clare. Tel. (061) 364082; fax (061) 364350.* This is an exquisite gourmet cellar restaurant, serving classic cuisine. Always bustling, it has plenty of clientèle to create an ambience for a memorable evening. Open Tue–Sat 7pm–4:30pm. Major credit cards.

Manuel's Restaurant €€ *Kilkee, Co. Clare; Tel. (065) 56211.* Modern restaurant, with nautical decor, specializing in seafood and shellfish, and lovely vegetarian dishes. Open daily from Easter to mid-Sept, 6:30–10:30pm. Major credit cards.

Ireland

Waterford

Dwyer's €€ *8 Mary Street, Waterford; Tel. (051) 877478.* Small gourmet restaurant with limited but original menu that changes every two weeks. Closed Sunday. Major credit cards.

Grand Hotel €€ *Tramore, County Waterford; Tel. (051) 381414; fax (051) 386428.* Excellent hotel; its main restaurant has a panoramic view of the sea. Extensive menu. Major credit cards.

Ship €€ *Dock Road, Dunmore East; Tel. (051) 383141.* Fresh seafood served in informal surroundings. Closed Sun and Mon, and November–March. Major credit cards.

Wexford

Cellar Restaurant €€ *Horetown House, Foulksmills, Co. Wexford; Tel. (051) 565771.* A 300-year-old cellar, complete with log fire, specializing in country house cuisine. Major credit cards.

Captain Whites €€ *White's Hotel, George's Street, Wexford; Tel. (053) 22311; fax (053) 45000.* Delicious country farm-house-style food. Major credit cards.

Marlfield House Hotel €€ *Courtown Road, Gorey Co. Wexford; Tel. (055) 21124; fax (055) 21572.* An interesting mix of French and Irish cuisine; menu includes selection of fish dishes; classic, country house setting. Major credit cards.

Wicklow

Hunter's Hotel €€–€€€ *Newrath Bridge, Rathnew, County Wicklow; Tel. (0404) 40106; fax (0404) 40338; e-mail <reception@hunters.ie>.* An historic 18th-century coaching inn with fine gardens; specializes in exquisite cooking. Major credit cards.

Old Rectory Country House & Restaurant €€ *Wicklow Town, County Wicklow; Tel. (0404) 67048 fax (0404) 69181.* Fine, imaginative cooking often made or garnished with edible herbs or flowers. Closed Jan–Feb. Major credit cards.

Recommended Restaurants

Pizza del Forno € *The Mall Center, Main Street, Wicklow Town; Tel. (0404) 67075.* Excellent family restaurant, with red checkered tablecloths. Serves pizzas, steaks, and vegetarian food. Closed Chirstmas–mid-Feb. Major credit cards.

The Roundwood Inn €€ *Main Street Roundwood, Bray, Co. Wicklow; Tel. (01) 281 8107.* Menus influenced by German cuisine. Also serves good bar food, featuring goulash, Irish stew, smoked salmon. Open Tues–Sat 1pm–2:30pm, 7:30pm–9:30pm. Major credit cards.

Northern Ireland

Bananas €€ *4 Clarence Street, Belfast BT2 8DX; Tel. (02890) 339999.* Friendly restaurant with tropical ambiance serving such specialities as lamb kebab, tiger prawns and chicken kiev. Closed Sundays.

La Belle Epoque €€ *61/63 Dublin Road, Belfast BT2 7HE; Tel. (02890) 323244; fax (02890) 323244.* Classic French gourmet restaurant; serves game in season. Major credit cards.

Portaferry Hotel €€ *10 The Strand, Portaferry, Co. Down BT22 1PE; Tel. (012477) 28231; fax (02847) 28999; <www.portaferryhotel.com>.* Quayside spot for fresh seafood, including stuffed mussels, fried oysters, and turbot. Also bar food. Major credit cards.

Roscoff Restaurant €€ *7 Lesley House, Shaftesbury Square, Belfast BT2 7DB; Tel. (02890) 331532.* The city's most famous gourmet restaurant, in the French tradition, serving such delights as crispy duck confit and tasty roast sikka venison. Closed Sunday. Major credit cards.

Slieve Donard Hotel €€ *Downs Road, Newcastle, County Down BT33 0AH; Tel. (028437) 23681; fax (028437) 24830; <www.hastingshotels.com>.* The Peray French Inn at the entrance to the hotel is a welcoming and popular venue, serving pub lunch and dinner fare. Major credit cards.

INDEX